Sailing

From Jibs to Jibing

BOOKS BY GARY PAULSEN
WITH JOHN MORRIS

Canoeing, Kayaking and Rafting
Hiking and Backpacking

Sailing

From Jibs to Jibing

Gary Paulsen

Illustrated by Ruth Wright Paulsen

JULIAN MESSNER
NEW YORK

Manufactured in the United States of America.

Design by Irving Perkins Associates

Library of Congress Cataloging in Publication Data

Paulsen, Gary.
  Sailing, from jibs to jibing.
  Bibliography: p.
  Includes index.
  Summary: The author offers instructions with his
personal touch on sailing basics, including advice
on care, equipment, repair, and emergency procedures.
  1. Sailing—Juvenile literature. [1. Sailing]
I. Paulsen, Ruth Wright, ill. II. Title.
GV811.P34   797.1′24   81–9627
ISBN 0–671–34057–3   AACR2

Contents

Introduction

To move with the power of the wind, to feel the smooth, steady surge that comes with capturing and holding the natural forces of wind, water, and movement and bringing them together to take you where you want to go, whether for pleasure or work—sailing is more than just another way to get from one point to another, more than just another sport.

In fact, when you talk to people who sail, you rapidly come to the conclusion that sailing is (a) a way of life, (b) an art form, and/or (c) a whole mystical and semi-spiritual philosophy that can govern your life, a philosophy so secret it even has its own language, wherein a rope is called a *sheet*.

And in truth, sailing is all of that, or can be. Whether you are in a 75-foot schooner or a sailing canoe, it can be a way of life, a concept for living that is natural and clean. When you sail you take nothing from nature; you merely borrow the force of the wind or tap it temporarily. No energy is wasted, no resources are consumed.

As for its being an art form, it is only necessary to do it once to see the beauty in it, the grace and flow and power. There are many other art forms that will never

7

SAILING: *From Jibs to Jibing*

be able to duplicate the beauty that comes naturally with sailing.

But with this mystical quality there also arises a common mistake about sailing that is the real reason for this introduction and, as a matter of fact, the whole book: because it is so magical, many people who have never sailed have come to believe that sailing is difficult to learn. Many feel sailing takes too much strength, or too much coordination—or that it takes too large a commitment in time or money.

Actually, it is just the opposite. Sailing is probably one of the easiest sports of all to learn, requires much less strength than you'd think (less than volleyball, for instance), and can be learned in a few hours. As far as money is concerned, it depends on what you want to do. If you're thinking of a single-handed circumnavigation of the world in a 30- or 40-footer, or cruising the Pacific for a few years, you're going to get into a chunk of money—up to a hundred thousand dollars or more.

The money involved is minimal, however, if you're just going to learn to sail for fun, or to get around on your favorite fishing lake, or to take a sailing-camping trip. You can rig up your own boat, make the whole thing, for less than the price of a ten-speed bike. You can whip down to the marina and rent a boat for a few hours without spending a fortune, or you can help clean a dock and sail for nothing, if you work it right.

It is difficult to describe sailing until you do it. Maybe it would be better to let you form your own opinion.

8

I have lived in a sailboat on the Pacific Ocean two different times and have sailed up and down the West Coast. There were moments of such beauty that they almost stopped my heart. But one particular moment comes back: when I was sailing back from the offshore islands in the evening. There was a good wind, perhaps 20 knots, which is what it took to drive my 26-footer well. I was taking the wind just over my left shoulder into full-bellied sails that caught the gold of the setting sun and washed me in yellow light. I had the rudder under the crook of my knee and I was sipping coffee and I looked out over the bow and caught my breath. I was sailing down a lane of gold fire on the water, the path of the sun's reflection going out ahead of me and coming from behind me. The wind was creaming me along, and two dolphins—two free and beautiful and wonderful dolphins—came up out of the gold ahead of me, up and up into the clean light of the sun spinning in a glorious golden spray of beauty so stunning that it is still frozen in my mind.

Sailing is more than what is written in this book. No two people get the same exact joy from sailing. Part of it is part of you, somehow, as a person, and if you get hooked on your first go at sailing—as most people do—what happens and the beauty you find will depend on you as well as sailing itself.

Sailing is a way for you to dance with the wind and the water.

Chapter One

Getting Started

What you need to start sailing is pretty simple: some wind, some water, a boat with sails, and some form of steering. And a life jacket. When you *start* to learn to sail you might as well accept one primary, vital, and important fact: you are going to tip over. It will happen. No matter how stable you think the boat might be (assuming it isn't a clipper ship), it will tip over and you will get dumped, so always wear a life jacket. And know how to swim and handle yourself thoroughly in the water. Sailboats are meant to tip a certain amount, and indeed they go the fastest and cleanest when they are tipped a bit (it's called *heeling*). The whole trick in sailing fast is to learn to control that tip, that heeling over, and while you're learning, if you go a bit too far—which you inevitably will—you go right on over. It's no big thing, but you will get dunked, so safety first. Know how to swim and always wear a good life jacket that is the correct size for your weight.

To start actually sailing, the next thing after you get a life jacket is to acquire a boat in one way or another. This means that before we get into the specifics of harnessing wind and water, we'll have to deal with finding a boat.

In all honesty, almost anything will sail, given enough wind. You don't even need sails, if you have enough wind. I once sailed 40-odd miles at 6 knots on just the hull of my boat with no sails up when the wind was very strong.

You can take an ordinary 12-foot rowboat and rig up a sail with some pipe and a sheet and clamp a piece of plywood on the side for a keel and lash a canoe paddle to the stern for a rudder and it will sail. Not well, not fast, but it will actually sail and help to teach you how to do the basic maneuvers—so don't get caught in the trap of thinking it's going to take a lot of money or special equipment to get started.

Most people who start sailing, however, start with a proper sailboat and usually with something small, easy to handle, and fairly stable. There are some boats—like the sailing surfboards—which seem to flip if you exhale on the sail, and while you can learn to sail on such a craft, it might be easier on something firmer.

It's futile to go into brand names or descriptions of the various boats, but if you look for something with a relatively small sail, a single sail (to start with), and not over 10 or 12 feet long—even 8 if you can find it—you'll find things a bit easier until you learn what's going on. When the wind jams the boat against the dock, or when you capsize (repeatedly), or when the wind drives you

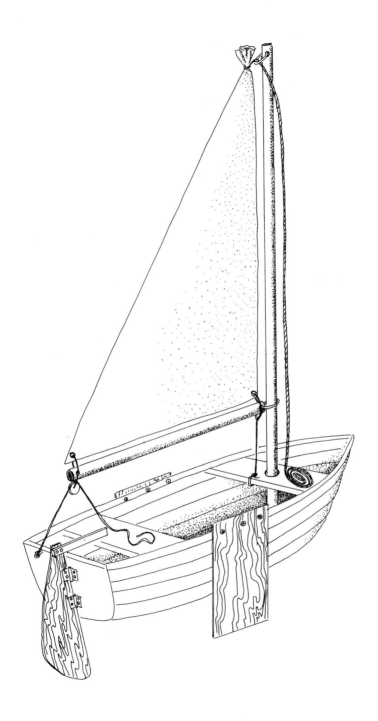

SAILING: *From Jibs to Jibing*

up on the shore, a smaller boat is physically easier to handle.

Look for something rather beamy—wide and with a roundish bottom. Long, sleek, fast-and-deadly-looking boats are perhaps a bit more elegant, but they also demand more skill to sail and will dump you faster than you can believe. If you get something slightly wide, you'll find it easier to handle while you learn.

Where you look for a boat to learn to sail, or how you go about it, depends on you and your abilities. If you can borrow one from a friend it will save money, or if you've got a rich uncle who thinks you just simply *must* have a sailboat of your very own, so much the better. But there are other methods.

Rental is one already mentioned, and usually you can rent a small sailboat at a marina or park for not too much money. It helps to look for the best deal, naturally, and in that sense you might avoid the heavy periods of rental activity. If you go down to the sea on a warm summer weekend or hit the lakeside on a Saturday afternoon in July, you'll have trouble renting a boat. But if you can get down there on a Wednesday morning, for instance, and tell the rental person that you're just learning and that you're not rich, there's a good chance he'll give you a break on a long-term (all-day) rental.

One person we talked to had a deal worked out with the marina whereby he helped out on the weekend for a few hours and had use of one of the boats for the rest of the week for no rental at all. This is worth a try and works more often than you'd think. Marinas usually need help during the peak weekend hours and if they can get it for simply letting you use a boat, they don't have to spend any actual money. Then, too, you get the added benefit of learning from all those people you help. You can learn a fantastic amount about sailing simply by watching others go at it—whether they be good or bad sailors. If you see somebody tip over twenty-three times in a row before he's 30 yards from the dock, you can be relatively certain he's doing something wrong. And if you notice this same person sitting on the downwind side of the boat so that his weight adds to the tipping motion of the boat (heeling) rather than subtracts from it, you've got your first and one of the most vital lessons. Always sit on the upwind side of the boat so that your weight keeps it from capsizing. While that sounds amazingly simple, it is surprising to go to a marina and watch how many new sailors have trouble learning this basic point.

But to get back to getting a boat—rental isn't the only way. If you have some money you can buy one flat out, although you'll have to have a pretty substantial amount if you're considering a new boat. In sailing, people seem to have a massively inflated idea of a boat's worth. If you take a standard little 8-foot dinghy, made from glass or wood or both, you can pick it up with the oars for not too much money, especially if it's used. But throw a little rag on for a sail and add a rudder and a bit of sideboard made from the cheapest plywood and the exact same boat—now termed a "sailing dinghy"—is suddenly worth up to five times as much. So look for a cheap one or, better yet, one that's in need of repair. If it hasn't actually been run over by a truck, it's quite easy to repair boats, if you don't mind a lot of hard work and sweat (see Chapter Fourteen). Often those same rental places will have boats that have been damaged or worn past what they consider fixable, worn to where they can logically call them a business write-off, take the tax depreciation, and get new ones. But they'll still be completely good boats with a little work on your part.

You could also take a standard dinghy or small boat and put sails on it. If you can scrounge around and find a small boat or dinghy for not too much money, say one that's in bad need of repair, you have a start. Again, if you don't mind some sweat and some work, it's quite easy to fix a boat up, add your own mast, sails, and rigging, rudder, and sideboards and you have a sailboat. When you consider that dinghies often get banged up and can be picked up cheap—on many occasions I have found them abandoned on beaches—you can see how inexpensive it is to come by a boat this way.

Some good people to get to know if you're looking for wrecked but repairable dinghies or small boats are insurance adjustors. They're always running into blitzed small boats and will sometimes "sell" them to you for a dollar or two just to clear them off the books and get rid of the junk. Call around to a few of them and give them your name and tell them to keep you in mind for anything that comes along in glass or wood small boats that have been wiped out. It doesn't always pay off, but it may come through.

Finally, you can make a small sailboat from scratch. While it may sound scary and may take a little time and effort, it really isn't all that hard to do if you have a moderate amount of hand-eye coordination. There are many people who, faced with the stunning expenses of buying new and completely rigged-out boats, make their own sailboats from scratch. Not a few of them make really *big* boats—ocean-going rigs that sleep six, that sort of thing.

If you can't find a junker, can't afford a rental, can't find a rental that will allow you to work it off, haven't got a rich uncle, and just simply *can't* find a way to get a boat for a time, take heart. You aren't done in yet.

Check the yacht clubs around the marinas and try to get on as a crew member on some of the racing boats. These are not necessarily big boats; they are usually just small ones with the owner (the "captain") and one crew member—you. Put your name on the bulletin board at the club for crewing, explain that you have little or no experience and need the training, and you'll probably find yourself working a jib sheet (the rope that controls the front sail on a two-sail boat, called a *sloop*) in no time at all. There is some strain to being a crew member during a race, because it is, after all, a race—often the language can get a little loud and heavy. It's awesome how seriously some of those sailors take those races.

Racing will probably teach you to sail better than any other method. I learned to sail that way and I will never forget the feeling that came over me the first time I went out on a little 20-footer, working the jib sheets, and had the "captain" tear a strip off me for moving too slow. He did a good job of it, left my ears and the hair above them smoking, and I was going to mutiny until I realized that I'd *asked* to crew on his boat. After a time, the first leg of the race, I just closed my ears to the hard parts and did as I was told and was absolutely leveled when I found we'd won our class in the race—I couldn't believe it. As it turned out, the man who was the owner-captain of the boat was a master sailor. He had sailed twice from Los Angeles to Sydney, Australia, and over the next several months he taught me so well that I still often use things he showed me. At one point later in my life, I was out on the Pacific in my 26-footer with my wife and son and we got caught in something very near a hurricane with 80-knot winds and driving seas, and for one brief moment I saw my death coming—at that time, what this man taught me about how to come about (turn around) in driving seas saved my life and the lives of my wife and son. That's how much I learned racing, and it was well worth any possible verbal abuse I might have suffered.

As a last note on the business of acquiring a boat for learning to sail: it is best to avoid any boat about which you aren't too sure of the ownership papers. In small boats particularly there is a lot of movement in stolen boats. For all the obvious reasons, they should be avoided. If you buy or get one that way, it can be taken away from you, and you might get nailed as an accessory. But putting moral and legal issues aside for the moment, if you work with a hot boat it can flavor and cheapen the whole concept of sailing for you. Learning to sail, learning to dance with the wind and the water, is such a beautiful and clean thing, such a wonderful bit of joy, that bringing it down by dealing with a stolen boat can ruin most of the happy part of sailing for you.

And nothing should do that.

Chapter Two

Moving on the Water

Sailing is easy, straightforward, and basic. Just sailing. It means you are going to get on the water and be propelled by the wind. That's all. If you sit in a washtub and hold your arms up with a pillowcase between them and enough wind hits the pillowcase you will sail. Not for long, and you will most assuredly get flipped and sink, but you will sail for a time, no matter how brief.

The trick in sailing is to use the wind to take you where *you* want to go, not just where the wind drives you. The washtub and pillowcase are probably like the early so-called sailing boats, the primitive ones used by early tribes, which would scud ahead of the wind with crude sails of mat or skins. There is movement with such a boat but no steering, and the direction depends entirely on luck—you go where the wind goes.

Clearly, more is needed to get correct sailing, with steering and purpose, and before getting into actual application, some understanding of what happens when a boat is under sail is necessary.

There are very complicated formulae involved in mathematically explaining what happens when a boat sails—long, involved things that deal with Force A (wind) against Force B (water) and the keel and hull design and the heel of the boat and the center of gravity and where the mast is set and at what angle it rakes back and the shape of the sail and the material of the sail and the weight of the cargo and the way the cargo is distributed and the size and direction of the waves and the kind of rigging . . .

It has reached the point where it's virtually impossible to understand what sailing is all about by looking at the formulae. Such explanations usually come equipped with at least eight drawn arrows showing wind and water pushing at various angles with all sorts of curves and vector-force lines that really serve only to confuse.

Point: A boat sails because the wind pushes it. Period.

All other explanations are unnecessary at the moment, unless you are going into hull design or marine engineering, in which event you'll need much more than this book as a text.

The wind pushes the boat. It never pulls. And that's all that counts. You can never go straight up into the wind, only at an angle to it, no matter how wild your theory becomes.

Any boat will sail. An old clunker rowboat with no oars or paddles will drive before the wind if you put a sail on it—straight before the wind, and that's all. But it's sailing, and all it needs is some way to obtain steering and it will be the same sailing as that done by the Vikings or Columbus.

The main point to keep in mind about steering for the moment is that water is much "harder" than wind— the liquid won't compress. If your boat is moving straight downwind under sail and you drop a wall that is bolted to the boat down into the water, what happens?

The boat stops—and will tip over with the push of the wind (keep that tipping in mind for later). Now with the wind pushing straight one direction and the wall holding straight back against the water, nothing will happen except that the tip will increase until all the wind is spilled off over the tipped sail (a condition known as *blow-down*).

If, however, you slightly angle the wall under water so it isn't straight across the wind but angled one way or the other, the boat will move off at an angle, will kind of "squirt" off to the side.

You have steering. The boat is no longer moving only downwind but slightly off to the side. It is this basic concept, this business of water being "harder" than wind, and the wall down in the water that control all sailing of all boats and sailing ships, that give steering to all wind-driven boats and ships, and are the basic principles of sailing.

The wind pushes against the sail, the "wall" down in the water is the keel, and the rudder, a variable steering device on the stern, allows you essentially to angle the wall one way or the other to make the steering variable. It is that simple, that basic.

Unfortunately, the above-mentioned concepts, as dis-

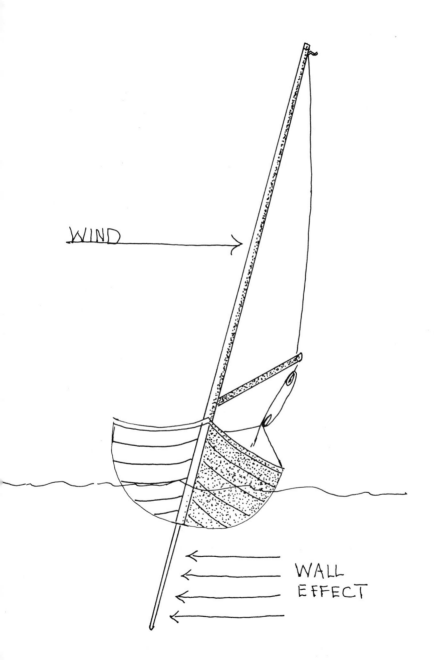

WIND

WALL
EFFECT

cussed so far, allow you to sail only downwind. It is interesting to note that for many centuries, before they discovered the idea of putting the wall down in the water—putting a keel on a boat—all they could do was sail downwind. For hundreds of years, even the larger ships could only move with the wind, and any voyages made were dependent entirely on wind direction. Often the crews had to wait weeks and months for the wind to change so they could go home.

But then came the keel and a strange thing happened to the wind. It was found that when the keel was down in the water and the wind pushed against the sail from the side, it "bent" the wind and changed the direction of push. This might not have meant much except that they found that because of this bending action in the force of the wind, it was possible not only to sail off to the side downwind but also straight across the face of the wind and even up into the wind a bit.

They couldn't go directly against the wind, but they could angle up into it so that if they went back and forth at this angle for a time, the end result was that they averaged out to be going against the wind. (This maneuver is called *tacking*.) It took a lot longer to get where you wanted to go than running downwind, and it's a bit rougher because you have to sort of buck the wind and water movement, and it slams the hull, but it was better than waiting two or three months for the weather patterns to change the wind direction.

Nobody has ever been able to sail straight up into the

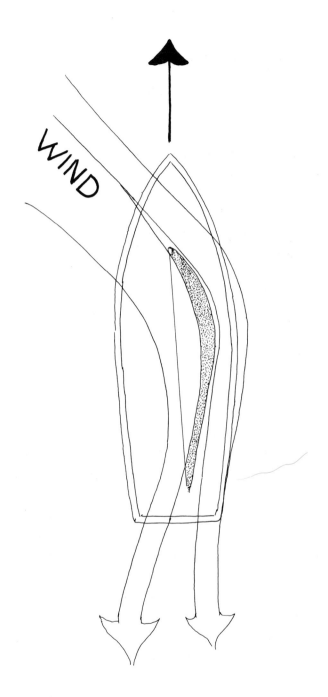

WIND

wind, but tacking has allowed people to move against the direction of the wind and has made sailing probably the most efficient use of energy. The big ships weren't too good at tacking because their keels didn't go down in the water very far, but small boats with straight-down and flat keels of plywood can tack very well. Some of them can point up into the wind to within 45 degrees of the direction of the wind (this is called *pointing ability*), but all boats are different, even boats of the same basic design. Later we'll cover how to find your boat's best tacking (pointing) ability.

Sailing is overloaded with special terminology. Every sail has its own name—and when you get into those old huge square-riggers with dozens of sails it can get pretty wild—as does every other part of the boat and all the various maneuvers involved with moving the boat.

Since quite a few of these names date back to ancient times, they don't all make sense in modern terms, and it can be pretty confusing for somebody just starting out. Pulleys, for instance, are called *blocks* because they used to use wooden blocks with holes drilled in them as pulleys. Ropes are called *sheets* when they control the sails. Speaking of sails, it's relatively easy to see why they call the big middle sail the *mainsail*, but when you learn that the front sail is called the *jib* and the rear sail, if any, is called the *mizzen*, or why a boat with a single sail is a *sloop* and one with three arranged a certain way is a *ketch*

—new sailors have been known to break down under the sheer weight of the verbiage.

Then, when you add in slang and find that really salty sailors call their sails *rags* and their masts *sticks,* so that when a sailor tells you "The wind come up so I jerked my rags and took the storm with my bare sticks," it's supposed to mean something—it can definitely put a crack in your serenity.

The point, of course, is that much of the terminology —perhaps most of it—isn't really necessary. Whether you call it a block or a pulley or a sail or a rag doesn't matter as much as knowing how to use these things to sail your boat. It's only when talking to other sailors and when you want to be impressive that you need to know most of those special terms.

On the other hand, there are some special words that are universal and are always used, and it is helpful to keep those in mind, if only to make later descriptions in this book easier to follow. The basic terms have to do with the direction of movement when you're sailing. Some of them are listed below, and it would help to know them before going on.

Sailing straight downwind (in the same direction as the wind) is called *wing and wing* because when you have two sails you put one out to one side and the other to the other; it is about the slowest way to sail and yet the most beautiful, because the sails belly out so grandly.

Across the wind is the fastest way to sail and is called *reaching*, with special qualifying terms; straight across

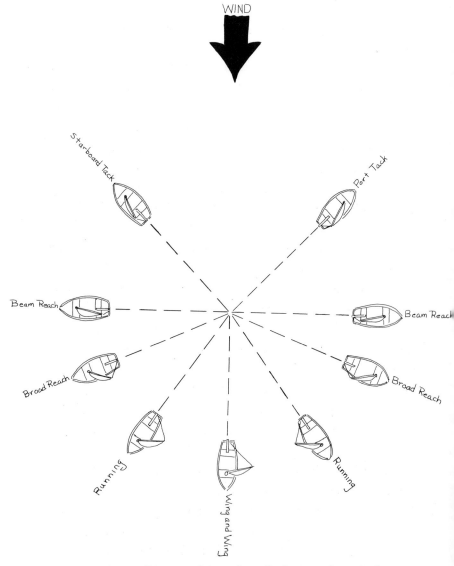

Various sailing positions in relation to the wind.

the wind is called a *beam reach* because the wind is coming right across the middle or beam of the boat. If you move away from the direction of the wind, moving towards going downwind just a little, it's called a *broad reach* and is truly a glorious way to sail. It all comes together in a broad reach, the whole concept of sailing, the driving of a boat through the water with the power of the wind. Some of the old clipper ships, towering in sail, would hit the trade winds just right and be on a broad reach for thousands of miles as they crossed the oceans.

Moving into the wind, as already discussed, is called *tacking*, or *moving to windward*. For obvious reasons it is a slow way to sail, although while you're doing it the pace seems very fast because you're bucking the wind and the water movement, and you get the illusion of speed. In larger boats, on big lakes or especially the ocean, this is a very rough way to sail, with much water spraying back on you and great pounding of the hull as it slams into the waves. *Pointing*, as previously mentioned, is a way to describe how close a boat will sail into the wind; a boat that "points high" is one which will go closer into the wind than one that "points low." The measure of a sailor is also how high he or she can get a boat to point up into the wind and still move forward. It takes true skill and understanding of the forces involved to point a boat really high.

Port means left and *starboard* means right. This is because the left side of the boat was typically towards port when at anchor and the right side of the boat was used when shooting the stars with a sextant for navigation at sea.

So, when you move off to the right on a tack to windward it's called a *port tack*, because the wind comes over the left side of the boat and when you move off to the right it's called a *starboard tack*, because the wind comes over the right.

It's all quite simple and easy to follow, although all the maddening terms can be a bit rattling at first. Think in terms of the clock, as illustrated, and keep in mind that none of the terms is that important except as a way of describing what to do.

All that matters is that you learn how to sail and have a good time doing it. Everything else, all the terminology and cute "in" phrases, is secondary.

In a way it's like knots. Almost all books ever written about sailing (except this one), have whole chapters, whole sections on tying knots. To further compound the problem, these knots have their own terminology and strange names—even stranger than the naming of the sails and parts of the boat. There is a whole world based on knots, a whole mystique, and in some sailing schools the first thing they have the students do is sit down and start working at knots. Some of these schools won't let their students *sail* until they learn to tie and untie a certain specified number of knots.

To be honest, at one time it was necessary to know knot tying to sail a boat or ship. In the old days it was

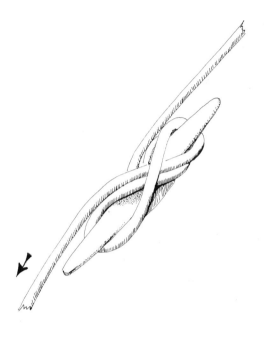

necessary to tie ropes off with special quick release knots and tie sheets off to hold the sails. But now it is possible to sail a small boat or a large one, for that matter, without ever having to tie a knot other than to hang your laundry. Using various cleats—small two-armed things that hold the rope and jam cleats, which pinch and hold rope—you can do nicely with almost no knots at all.

If you want to learn all the knots and specialized terms, fine, but don't let them scare you away from sailing. They aren't truly necessary.

Chapter Three

The Boat

Before actually climbing into a boat and getting onto the water, it is necessary to take a look at the tool you will use: it is necessary that the boat become an extension of you, almost a physical part of your body and mind. The only way to make that happen is to understand the boat completely. This chapter is intended to familiarize you with a small sailing boat.

Boats are very much like people. No two are quite alike, even two of the same make and design, and differently designed boats do different things. A flat-bottom boat, for instance, will seem to be stable and will ride level even when pushed with a side wind, and then will instantly—when it reaches a certain point—flip over and capsize. A round-bottom boat, or one with curved sides on the hull, seems to be *not* stable and tends to roll over on its side easily. Yet it won't capsize as easily because a round-bottom boat is inherently more stable than a flat-bottom boat.

Yet there are similarities, no matter the kind of boat. They all have a sail, which provides the power from

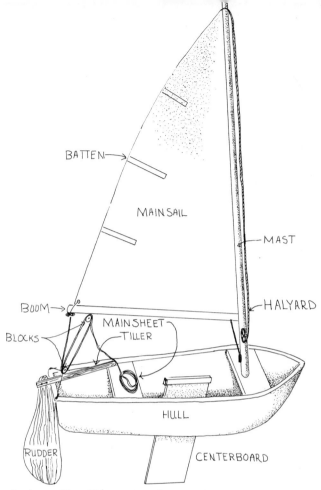

BATTEN

MAINSAIL

MAST

BOOM

HALYARD

MAINSHEET

BLOCKS

TILLER

HULL

RUDDER

CENTERBOARD

A typical small sailboat showing various parts.

the wind to move the boat. Nowadays, the sail is usually
made of synthetic material, fairly dense to keep the air
from moving through it. There is a rope to pull the sail
up called the *uphaul* and also *halyard* (another one of
those terms); there is a rope to hold the sail down to
keep it tight along the edge, called a *downhaul*; and
there is a rope to pull the sail out to keep it tight along
the bottom edge, called an *outhaul.* Up along the outside

edge of the sail are some little sticks called *battens*. These are to stiffen the edge of the sail and make it use the wind more efficiently.

The sail goes up the *mast*. In one of those few sensible things you'll find in sailing terminology, the top of the mast is called the *head* and the bottom is the *foot*. The arm sticking out to the side holding the bottom of the sail is called the *boom*.

The main body of the boat is the *hull*, and the front of the boat is the *bow*, and the rear is the *stern*. You can also call it the front and rear, if you like.

The *rudder* is the device at the rear for steering the boat, and the handle of the rudder is called the *tiller* or *helm*.

The *keel* is the device that drops down through the middle and acts as a wall to keep the boat from sliding sideways across the water. This is also called the *centerboard* and *daggerboard*, and without it, the boat will only sail straight downwind.

Everything else is pretty much self-explanatory except the rope that controls the boom and the sail. This is called the *mainsheet*, because it is the rope that controls the mainsail on boats with more than one sail. Later in the book we'll be talking about sailing boats with more than one sail, each one having its own set of sheets, but for now just the one is enough. The mainsheet is put through a couple of pulleys (*blocks*) because the force of the wind on the sail exerts too much power to handle easily without the help of pulleys.

If you understand a small boat and can sail a small boat, you can understand and sail a huge schooner. The principles are exactly the same, the forces are the same, and the movements are the same. There is a true saying in sailing that states the larger the boat, the easier it is to sail. It is much harder to sail a small dinghy or boat than it is a big cruiser. The small boat tips more easily, for starters, and is harder to get to work with light winds, for another, and if you can get an 8-footer to work right for you you'll have no trouble later with a 30- or 40-footer.

Before getting into actual sailing, lean back and look at the picture of the boat and think of what things do and are for. Mentally put yourself in the boat and on the water with a wind.

There is a tendency, the first time you sail, for everything to go wrong—we'll cover that in a later chapter. But if you mentally visualize what will happen when you're in the boat, make the boat a part of you now in your mind, it can do a great deal to minimize any later problems.

First, think of sitting in the boat on the water. It will not be still. There will be movement, rocking with small waves, moving with the wind—a good boat is never still until it's tied up at the dock. It moves because it's *supposed* to move, it's supposed to be light and move across the water easily with the lightest of breezes. Expect the movement and have the feeling of moving, imagine becoming a part of it, swiveling at the hips to compensate for it, to fit your body to it. It is very important that you make the boat an extension of yourself if you're really going to enjoy sailing. You must fit into the movements of the boat the way good riders fit into the movements of the saddle when they ride a horse.

While we're discussing movement, take another look at the sail and the mast and visualize how they work together. As the wind pushes at it the sail takes the force against the cloth and the whole thing, the sail and mast and boom, becomes a kind of moving lever. It won't bend very much, so something has to give.

Obviously, the boat is what gives. It moves across the water, but more important, for the moment, it tips. The sail acts as a large arm with the wind for the muscles and it tips (*heels*). Now visualize what happens when it tips. The boat itself moves towards sitting up on its edge—and some boats will actually hang right there on their edge for a time before capsizing.

Now, still looking in your mind at the tipping boat, what can you do to eliminate the tipping? Or at least control it? Sit on the "high" side and let your weight be a counterbalance against the push of the wind. This is one of the most fundamental aspects of sailing small boats: keep your weight on the high side, the side the wind is coming from, with your back to the wind.

Sitting on the "low" side is also the most common mistake made in sailing small boats, or in learning to sail them. In fact, it is mind-boggling to see how many people climb into a small sailboat and sit on the low

side—which adds their weight to the push of the wind—
and then wonder why they spend so much time tipping
over and getting dunked.

Think of the movements and forces involved and you
can see quite readily where you must sit to keep the
boat from going on over, to use your weight to the most
advantage.

The last kind of wind movement to consider is the
kind caused by the wind on the sail—the movement of
the sail and the boom. Clearly, when the wind pushes
against the sail the boom will move. The only thing
keeping it from moving is the rope tied to the end of
it, the main sheet, and if that's loose and the wind hits
the sail, the boom will definitely move. It will sweep
across the boat and pop your head, if you aren't ready
for it.

On big sailing boats and ships, that sweeping motion
of the boom when the wind hits the sails and the sheet
is loose can be devastating. Men have been killed by
it, and not a few times swept overboard. And while it
won't be nearly that bad on a small boat it can give your
head a lump or two, so watch it. When the main sheet
is loose and the wind is jigging around and changing
directions a lot (called "being fluky"), the boom comes
alive with movement. Keep your eye on it at all times
when sailing and remember to hold your head below
the level as it comes over.

The rudder moves as well, moves with wind and water
and your own power. As you visualize the boat and its

movements you can see that the rudder will move and that its movement will do something. The rudder turns the boat. If you pull the rudder handle to the left (port) side of the boat, it will turn the boat to the right, and if you pull it to the right (starboard), it will move the boat to the left.

This steering movement, along with your control of the main sheet on the mainsail, is the only control you have over the movement of the boat, and all you will need to sail it. So review it and memorize it and have it burned into your mind so that it's automatic *before* you go sailing, just as you would know how to use a steering wheel before you try to drive a car.

Pull it left, the boat goes right; pull it right, the boat goes left.

At last we come to the sail.

When the wind hits the sail the boom moves and the boat tips, but also the sail itself moves: the cloth bellies out, makes a curve, lets the air slide off, bellies out, makes a curve, lets the air slide off, and so on.

If the wind is gusty this happens rapidly and the sail makes a "luff-luff" sound as it whips and pops in the wind. Aptly, this whole thing is called "luffing," and it's something to be ready for when you start to sail. The sound can be a bit rattling if you don't expect it.

In fact, now, before you get into a boat and start to sail, might be the best time to get ready for all the various surprises that will be coming at you.

It's all well and good to sit and clinically discuss sailing in the quiet of your living room, talking about wind forces, water forces, and movements of different kinds. An understanding of all these things is absolutely necessary.

But to go down to the dock the first time on a breezy afternoon and look at a small sailboat in action is something else again. If there's a good breeze kicking up, the sail will be cracking back and forth, and the boom will be slamming from side to side and the tiller will be jacking from one side to the other and there will be much luffing and slamming of wood and rattling of blocks as the wind slaps everything around because it's loose.

The first time I tried to sail a 30-footer, something very close to panic hit me. I remember sitting at the dock with the sails pounding the air over my head and the boom whipping back and forth like the devil's tail and the tiller slamming against my legs. I remember sitting in the middle of that potential disaster wondering if there was any way I could successfully learn to sail it.

But all the things that are happening—all the sounds and clanks and rattles and movements and tipping—have a good, logical basis for being. They are all part of the boat.

Chapter Four

T*b*e Water

Along with the boat there are two other facets of sailing that have to be understood before you can actually get into a boat and start sailing.

They are the wind, which will be covered in the next chapter, and the water.

The boat moves on the water; but truly understanding it as a part of your sailing experience and how it effects sailing can be a difficult thing to do.

When I first learned to sail slightly larger boats—this time a 22-footer—the old man who taught me, named George, tried to explain how to deal with large waves in ocean sailing. He called them "lumps" in the water.

"Whether from the rear or the front, always take the big lumps from the quarter, never straight on or straight away. That lets you use the power of the water and not fight it."

What he was saying was that in heavy seas always take the force of the wave at an angle, left or right front or left or right rear, and never head-on or tail-on. As in all things, he was right—that's the best way to work in large waves or swells.

But the first time I got caught out in the open sea in my boat, caught in a moderate storm, and saw some good sized "lumps" brewing up, it was all different. I was sitting in the cockpit looking up at the crests of waves, waves that looked so immense and powerful that I felt there was nothing I or my boat could do to keep from being smashed by them. It was a very humbling experience and yet, had I understood the waves and the action of the water better, had I listened to George, I would have known the truth. Which is that waves of such size aren't necessarily bad at all, indeed are normal for ocean sailing, and a boat just slides up and over them with ease if handled correctly.

In sailing small boats, while it's true that you will never run into 30- or even 20-foot waves or swells, understanding what the waves and water do, what things mean, can help you sail.

Take the following example. No matter what type of small boat you are sailing, there will be a keel sticking out the bottom, down for some considerable distance. This might be as much as 2 feet, so hitting shallow water, say only a foot or so deep, could be a problem. While it probably won't hurt the boat if the keel hits the bottom—unless it's bad rocks—the boat will most certainly capsize when the keel hangs up. So avoid shallow water.

The way to "read" shallow water is to look for unexplained ripples on the surface out ahead of the boat, especially ripples that are in just one spot or totally different from the surrounding water motion. It could either be fluky wind or shoal (shallow) water, so keep your eye on it for a time and if it seems to move then it's fluky wind. If it stays in the same place no matter what the wind and other water seem to be doing, it's probably shallow and should be avoided if possible. (In the next chapter we'll deal with what to do if it's fluky wind.)

If you're river-sailing, look for snags, underwater boulders, or obstacles that will catch the keel and dump you. These will appear as upward "bulges" in the water, sometimes rather broad swellings, and if you see such a place in the water avoid it because it's certain to be high enough to catch your keel.

In river-sailing, look also for sudden drop or "holes" in the water. These are caused by the water trying to get around a large underwater obstacle, one that is so close to the surface that the water can't get over it easily. There is a kind of underwater vacuum hole on the down-current side of such an obstacle, and this telltale hole points up-current right to the shallow obstacle, most often a ledge of some kind or long log.

Shallow water can look exactly like all other water, but sometimes you can tell if it's going to be shallow by looking at the bank. If the bank comes down in a long, gradual slope that turns into water, then it's a good bet that it will be shallow out for a ways from the shore. You shouldn't try to get too close to the edge with the keel down. (You can raise the keel and rudder and skim in the last little bit on the wind but you'll only have minimal control of the boat.)

If the shore drops abruptly and comes straight down into the water, then chances are it will continue on down for a ways and be relatively deep and you can sail close to shore. These things do not always hold true, but quite often they do and it can help if you're caught on new water you don't know very well.

Water reading can also tell you in very exact ways what the wind is doing, and what it will do in the future to you and your boat. This is covered in the next chapter.

In sailing small boats, it is most likely that waves will never be a consideration for you. Generally, small boats are sailed on calm or near-calm bodies of water too small for significant wave action to be generated.

For those who will be sailing on large lakes or doing coastal ocean sailing—just out past the surf—a brief discussion of waves and what they can do to your boat might be handy.

Except for strange cases—such as under the Golden Gate Bridge in San Francisco—the waves will always be moving in the same approximate direction as the wind.

The waves tell you the wind direction. More than that, they add their force to that of the wind. If you are tacking up against the wind—beating to windward— while you are pulling forward at an angle the wind also tends to push you back. So do the waves. Even small waves on a small lake will hit the boat and retard forward motion to some degree. For this reason if there are waves coming at you with the wind you'll find it easier to hold speed if you fall off the wind a bit and try not to hit the waves head-on. It will also be drier since when a boat hits the waves head-on, water is usually sprayed up over the bow and down on you.

If the wind is so severe that it could cause large waves on a large body of water—not counting the ocean and big boats—you shouldn't be out there. Period. Any hint of heavy winds or worse, a small craft warning, and you should get to shore and pull the boat out as soon as possible.

If you find yourself caught in such weather, with strong winds and large waves, and you are sailing a small boat, you are most definitely in a sticky situation. You are going to get very wet and you are going to get an exceptionally rough ride. (See chapter on boat handling for specific measures to take.) It does no good to fight large, powerful waves; you must bend to that power and work with it, not against it.

A general thought to keep in mind when dealing with water and sailing is: never fight the elements. Always work with them and not against them. Water is a vital third of sailing, and understanding it and how it works with the boat you are going to sail will greatly enhance the enjoyment you get from sailing.

Chapter Five

The Wind

"The worst part of working with the wind," an old sailor told me, "is that you never get enough of it."

While that isn't specifically true, it *does* seem to be the case more often than not. If you sail every week for fifty years, in small or large boats on small or large bodies of water, far and away the most noticeable thing will be the lack of wind. There never seems to be enough of it. It seems like every time you want to go out and sail you either get dead calm or are caught in light and fluky winds. This is most true if you want to *get* somewhere with the boat, like across a body of water.

In sailing, more than in almost any other endeavor, you are dependent on nature, on the natural flow of things. You can't make the wind, and when it comes, you can't make it do what you want. You must deal with it as it exists. You must become part of the wind. There is an old saying, that a sailor is a brother (or sister) to the wind. You must become a part of the natural flow of things to really get into sailing. The best way to do that is to know it.

Wind is simply a movement of air, and in sailing you

just tap some of the energy of this movement of air. But the *way* it moves can be vital to the sailor. Light winds can drive your frustration factor over the top of the scale, medium winds that are gusty and fluky can make sailing a series of jerks and starts and heavy winds or unexpected gusts can bring you up to date on how to hold your breath as you go over.

First let's look at light or nonexistent winds. The truth is that anybody can sail a boat in wind. But as another of those sayings puts it, it takes a real sailor to move a boat when there isn't any wind.

In sailing small boats, or large, as far as that goes, it is the effect of the movement of air you watch for, rather than the air itself. For light airs watch the water ahead. Look for riffled places, little wrinkles in the surface. Just smudges in the smoothness of the water. Such a smudge or riffle means there is movement of air in that area; you can get your boat over there by sculling (working the tiller back and forth to move the boat forward slightly) or finding another closer bit of wind. It is possible to sail quite well just working from riffle to riffle. Watch birds and insects too; they will often tell you where there is a bit of wind to use. Quite often light airs won't get down to the water to cause riffling but will get low enough to adequately hit the sails to cause movement. If birds or large winged insects are circling in an area, it usually means such a light off-surface wind exists: it is easier to fly with a little breeze.

Next study the shoreline, the trees, any smoke or heat

waves rising from buildings or parking lots. They will almost seem to shimmer in light airs; both smoke and heat ripple, shimmer, and bend with the wind. They can tell you that (a) there is wind, that (b) it will probably be coming onto the water off land soon, and (c) where you must be to catch and use it.

It is, however, best to avoid sailing too close to the shore in light airs. You may run aground, but the real problem is that wind tends to be worse right along the shore. There can be good wind on land, and good wind further out and it can still be calm right where the land turns to water. This is especially true if the banks are bluffy or have a sharp drop, because this more or less causes the wind to hump up and over to get on the water, leaving a void underneath right at the shoreline. This is a good thing to know if there is some strong wind coming—it will generally be weaker but gustier close to the shoreline.

A boat will sail in wind so faint that you almost can't feel it. It can seem to be dead calm, with flat water that looks like a hot mirror and even smoke seems to rise straight up. Yet there will be a touch of wind, a ghost of the tiniest puff or a wiffle, and a boat will sail on it.

If you can find it.

The problem with wind that light is that it leaves almost no sign—heat waves rise straight, trees don't bend, chimney smoke goes straight up through it. Some sailors put a few pieces of yarn in their pocket and when they think they are in dead calm they'll unravel just a bit of the lightest part of one string and stand up and release it and see if it moves off. If it does, they'll set their sails for a wind that follows the yarn, an almost imaginary wind, and in a minute or so the boat will start to move . . . slowly. Another thing that works is a piece of down or a particle of lint.

A last trick that is good if you're sailing by leafy trees on shore is to watch the leaves, not the whole tree. Certain leaves—like those of aspens—are almost critically balanced and will move in the tiniest bit of air movement. Watch the leaves and if they seem to shiver or quake there is wind along the shore.

Probably the most frustrating kind of wind—along with light airs—is what they call fluky wind. This is wind that might be gusty, or might be moderately strong or weak, but the worst thing about it is that it changes direction all the time and seemingly without warning.

Most often found in mountain lakes or along bluffy banks, such winds have been known to have the most experienced sailors tearing their hair out. The problem is that Ma Nature does what she wants, when she wants, and there isn't anything anybody can do about it. If there is fluky wind, then that is the wind you must sail to.

There are some things that can be done to lessen the frustration level and perhaps make some prediction possible. First, read the water ahead of the boat. Winds move the surface of the water in telltale ways, and if you're quick you can jump before the wind changes on you.

Let's say you're sailing along with the wind on your right cheek and you've been going that way for a hundred meters or so and up ahead you can see riffles on the water that seem to be pointing to the right. That means the wind up there is coming from the left and will hit you on the left cheek—completely opposite from the wind you're working at the present time. You're a jump ahead and you can get ready for a quick change on your sails and the effect won't be so sudden that the boom jumps over.

Watch those riffles. If they stay in the same place—as discussed in Chapter Four—they could mean shallow water. But if they move in relation to the shore, then they're caused by wind and will point in the direction the wind is blowing. Just watch the tips of the little waves and they'll lean away from the wind just like a sailboat.

But fluky wind doesn't always hit the water. As with light airs, it will often come down to just above the water, then skim along above the cold thermal layer that lies on the water surface and not disturb the water at all.

The problem is if you can't see any sign of it, how can you tell whether it's coming? Again, watch the birds. You can tell easily. Notice whether they are suddenly wheeling or zipping along on an unseen bit of wind. If, on the other hand, they're laboring hard to fly, then they're probably bucking a wind and that tells you not only that there is a wind and that it's coming from a certain direction, but also that it's a fairly stiff wind and you should get ready to take it.

Along with the birds, watch for sudden movements of insects. Dragonflies hunt flies and mosquitoes just over the water. If you watch them up ahead—they are large enough to see readily—and they suddenly get blown sideways, you know there's a gust. You won't have much of a warning, to be sure, but there will be some time to react, to move your body to the other side of the boat, and loosen the sheets.

Watch the shore for wind. It has to come from somewhere. Unless you're in mid-ocean, the wind you get comes from across the land and you can see its effect on the trees, chimney smoke, dirt, or dust before it gets to you.

Not only can you see the effect of the wind, but more importantly you can see the effect of a wind *change*. It is sudden wind changes—fluky wind—that makes sailing a challenge. Or gets you wet.

Strong gusts of wind are probably responsible for more capsizes than any other single element of sailing. To be certain, getting dunked and capsizing are part of sailing. But if you get whipped down nineteen times by unseen winds before you're 200 meters from the dock, it can definitely put a damper on your fun.

You attend to gusts—sometimes referred to as hammerwinds, snortwinds, putdown winds—the same way you watch for fluky winds. Read the water, the birds, the trees, the bugs—anything and everything around you. When a good gust hits a sparrow that's working just over the water, you can't miss it. One second the sparrow is there, the next he's gone. Trees will bend and straighten suddenly, insects disappear faster than birds, and the surface of the water where (and if) the gust sets down will look almost torn, sanded, chewed up.

A gust can come without touching down on the water, but there is a way to get a tiny warning. Just before it hits you will get a sudden sucking of wind towards the gust. It won't be violent, but it almost always comes. Say you're creaming along on a steady breeze heeled over slightly and an unseen gust is coming down on you. Just before it plows into you, the boat might straighten up a bit as the wind is pulled almost backwards into the coming gust. Just a quick straightening and then it's gone.

You just have time to react before it hits. Only moments. But it can be enough and you can let the sail out before you get knocked down.

Strong winds, steady and/or strong with stronger gusts take a great deal of skill to sail. They usually kick up the water into some pretty fair "lumps" and they have tremendous power. They can do just about as they wish to you and your boat. A good rule to follow, if at all possible, is to get off the water if you are aware that strong winds are coming. Beach the boat and ride it out on land, especially if you have a small boat or dinghy. In even moderately strong winds—and in any strong wind there is the potential for even stronger winds—it is very difficult to come through unscathed in a small boat.

Such winds will usually come with a thunderstorm, in which event you should immediately get off the water anyway. To be in a sailboat, especially one with an aluminum mast, is dangerous in a thunderstorm. If you see one coming, black rolling clouds building up with thunder and the odd jag of lightning, get off the water. Don't hesitate, don't wait. The problem is that just before such a storm hits, you get almost a dead calm. It's a real challenge to sail the light airs to get off the water before you get blitzed.

The only good thing about predicting strong winds, if anything, is that you can't miss them. They are easy to see coming and usually you will get enough warning to take your sails down and take appropriate action.

The power of the wind when it's strong is very evident—birds are blasted out of the sky, there are no bugs at all, trees and limbs are bending and waving, power lines are waving back and forth. If it's coming at you across the water, you will see the torn aspect of the water and waves—not too big, but "quick" (fast and choppy) —and if it's really a blow there might be spray whipped up a bit, although that's fairly rare.

Strong, unpredicted winds usually—you should always check the weather out with the weather service before going out—come with sudden thunderstorms or squalls, and there is something constant about them to hold in your mind. When the wind begans to "freshen" (an old sailing term) before the blow, it will move *towards* the front. This is that sucking action, the same one as in fluky winds and gusts, and what causes it is pretty simple.

The incoming front is like a huge wave coming onto shore. As it builds and rolls over on the top it pulls back along the bottom—call it a riptide of air, if you will—and so the wind is pulled along the bottom, where you and your boat are, towards the oncoming front.

This wind will be a bit temperamental, might be a bit strong, could be gusty, and will have swirls and eddies—just as a riptide does—and sometimes complete calms. But you can generally work this wind, sail it if you're careful, and use it to get to shore before you get hit by the more powerful wind that comes the other direction with the front or thunderhead. This can be overwhelming even if you're a good, experienced sailor, and can be devastating if you're just learning.

The one thing that should be clear about sailing and the use of the wind and the water is that there is no substitute for constant and intent observation.

To sail is to become part of nature, part of the cycle of forces that move all things, and you can't just fire up a 60-horse ski motor to get out of a jam—whether you're in a small boat on a lake or in a medium or large sailboat on the ocean. It is absolutely necessary that you watch things, all things at all times, keep your head and eyes moving, and "read" what is coming. Don't do it just when you're sailing, do it all the time, all year 'round. Study the weather and wind as you would study anything else you wanted to learn well. Work at it and *see* what it does. Become a brother to the wind.

The following is the international method of describing wind forces used by the national weather service. It is called the Beaufort Scale and you will hear it often in weather and wind reports.

Beaufort Scale	Weather Service	Wind velocity (miles per hour)
Force 0	Dead calm	0 to 1
Force 1	Light air	1 to 3
Force 2	Light breeze	4 to 7
Force 3	Gentle breeze	8 to 12
Force 4	Moderate breeze	13 to 18
Force 5	Fresh breeze	19 to 24

(At this point, between moderate and fresh breezes, it is time to examine the situation and perhaps head in until the wind goes down. This is a good cut-off point for small boats, a good safe area. When you have experience and a slightly larger boat, you can stay in until the next step and really enjoy it, but at first take it low and slow.)

Force 6	Strong breeze	25 to 31
Force 7	Moderate gale	32 to 38
Force 8	Fresh gale	39 to 46
Force 9	Strong gale	47 to 54
Force 10	Whole gale	55 to 63
Force 11	Storm	64 to 73
Force 12	Hurricane	74 and up

Chapter Six

Dumping;
Emergency Procedures

Before getting out on the lake or river and sailing, there is one more thing that needs to be covered and needs to be known so well that it's automatic: emergency procedures. What do you do when something or, more likely, everything, goes wrong. The first of these emergency procedures involves the one part of sailing that everybody eventually gets to do and nobody really wants to do.

Dumping. Going over. Capsizing.

As already mentioned, in sailing a small boat—or any boat without ballast (weight) down in the keel—sooner or later, the boat will get tipped over. The wind is capable of great and sudden strength, and without weight down on the keel to keep the boat upright (which all the larger boats have), the only control you have against the boat tipping is the distribution of *your* weight. You always sit on the upwind side, of course. But if a sudden wind reversal hits you before you have time to move to the other side, the boat is gone; your weight on the wrong side adds to the tipping power.

A lot of things happen fast when a boat goes over. First, the sails and mast come down to the water and—if the mast isn't buoyant or doesn't have a float on the end —might keep right on going until they hang down straight in the water. As might be imagined, this can prove to be a tricky situation because the mast and sail act like a huge wall underwater and resist any attempt to get them back up.

While the mast and sail are coming over and down, of course, you are not sitting idly by watching. Indeed, anybody in the boat is rapidly flipped out into the water. At this moment the only really possibly dangerous part of sailing can occur.

Do not, under any circumstances, allow yourself to become trapped under the sail as it comes down.

It can be a sopping wet, heavy, and dragging mess when it comes down, and while it won't literally drag you under if you're wearing a life jacket, the weight of the sail can push your head down a bit and might cause panic. Stay out from under it. If you should be caught unawares, don't panic. Hold your breath and work out to the side until you are free of the wet cloth, using your hands over your head to hold the cloth up as you work your way out. It's not a big thing, but it's the most critical part of capsizing and something you should watch out for when you go over.

As soon as the boat is over and you are clear of the

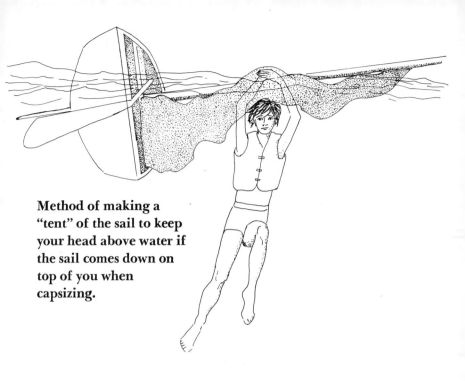

Method of making a "tent" of the sail to keep your head above water if the sail comes down on top of you when capsizing.

sail—actually, the sail hardly ever comes down on you—make certain any other people who were in the boat are clear and afloat and all right. Don't just use your eyes to check this out, because sometimes a person can momentarily look normal but have a throat full of water. Get them to tell you they are all right. Make them yell.

When you have made sure your passengers are all right, immediately begin the procedures for righting the boat. Move around to the bottom of the boat, edge up into the air, and climb up so you are standing on the centerboard. Your weight will bring the sail and mast back up out of the water—slowly on a larger small boat, but it will come—and you can then belly into the boat and bail the water out. The wind will quickly dry the sail while you're helping your friends back up into the

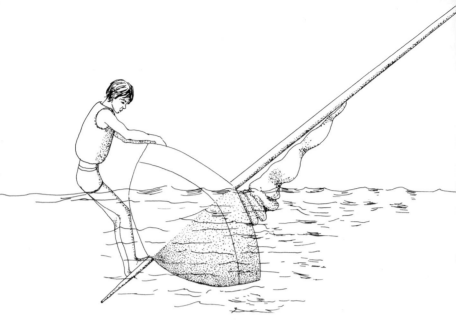

**Stand on the keel or centerboard to raise
the mast up out of the water.**

boat. While they are getting aboard, put your weight on
the opposite side of the boat, to counterbalance as they
belly over the side. but bail out the boat first (see Chapter
Seven).

The whole maneuver can be done in a couple of minutes. The wind will dry you out in a few more and you'll
be back to the fun part.

When you first go down to sail and the boat you're
going to use is sitting at the dock, leave her tied up on
a long rope from the bow, paddle her out with full sails
on until she's hanging on the rope and tip the boat over.
Make it capsize under control conditions and then right
it and bail it out and do it again. Do it several times so
you know what you're doing before you go out.

It might sound like a crazy thing to do, and people

**Climb over the rear transom to keep
the boat from tipping again.**

might think you're crazy for doing it. But capsizing is such an integral part of sailing a small boat that it's insane not to know how to handle the situation when it arises. The only way to truly know is to do it.

So . . . take her on over. Get wet. It might save you a lot of problems later when you have to do it in a high wind with some waves hammering at you. Know as much as you can ahead of time. In sailing, as in all things, knowledge is everything.

While covering capsizing, it is necessary to talk about wave action on people who are in the water. The reason you capsize is usually strong wind, and often strong wind can cause large waves. The problem with waves is that when you are in the water, a wave that looked like nothing from the boat looks huge when only your head is sticking up.

There is a potential danger in large or even medium-sized waves because they can break over your head. You will float out of them all right in a good life jacket, but for a moment now and then they might cover your head. This can be a bit startling if you don't know you're going to pop out right away.

Just be ready to get water on top of your head now and then. Don't try to breathe in regular patterns but take and hold breath whenever you get the opportunity. Hold your breath when the water is on you, exhale rapidly, and refill on air when the opportunity arises.

The primary rule in dealing with a capsized boat is the same for sailboats as for all boats—stay with the boat.

In those rare instances when the wind is too strong or the waves too choppy to allow you to get the boat back upright, *don't leave the boat* and try to swim to shore. Stay with the boat. All small boats will float even when full of water and keep you afloat as well. If, for some reason, you can't get the boat upright and back in sailing shape, just stay with it until somebody can pull you to shore.

Before you get towed in—being pulled in when the boat is full of water is called "being awash"—make every effort to get the boat upright or at least get the sail up out of the water. Do not tow the boat if the mast is sticking down, because as soon as it starts to get shallow the mast will be torn off.

Get it upright and then get in the boat—even if it's full of water—and help steer to shore. A sailboat doesn't pull very well and without steering will begin to oscillate in bigger and bigger movements until it flops over again. You have to steer it in. Sit well to the back, so your weight helps to hold the bow up, tie the tow rope to the front end and steer it in. While steering you might as well bail the boat out and get her floating again.

You might try to sail her again. Getting towed in lacks dignity, as one old sailor told me.

"She's meant to move on the wind, not some smoking cast-iron topsail [motor]. *Move* her on the wind," he said, spitting.

The first time you get towed you'll see what he meant. A sailboat that is a part of the wind under sail will turn into an ugly, rolling hog when being towed by a power boat. It's as if the sailboat objects to being towed.

It doesn't take long under tow to want to get under sail again.

Anytime you bring people and water together, in any form of endeavor, one primary danger always exists: drowning.

It is not a pleasant thing to think about, and if you take all the proper safety precautions, you will more than likely never come up against it, but the potential is there. The following procedures are put down for drowning aid.

Memorize them and practice them on a friend. In all probability you will never need to use them, but when and if you do, at that instant you must know them so well that you don't have to take time to think about them. When somebody is drowning or has apparently drowned, time is of the utmost importance. It is, literally, a matter of life and death. To waste time trying to remember the right way to help out can be enough to cause the situation to go bad.

Go over the list of things to do until they are fused in your mind and then get a friend to test you on them.

It's really that important.

First aid for drowning victims

1. Get to land or some flat surface as rapidly as possible.
   If you can't get to land or a dock, the front deck of a

good-sized boat will do, or, if nothing else, stretch the victim out flat on his back on the floor (bottom deck) of the sailboat. The main thing is to get him flat on his back with his face straight up.

2. Make certain the mouth is clear of any foreign substances (gum, seaweed, etc.). Be sure the tongue hasn't gone back in the throat, where it will block the passage of air. Keep the tongue in place on the floor of the mouth by placing your palm over the victim's chin and using your thumb to hold the tongue down.

3. With your other hand lift up on the neck so that the head is tilted back. (This straightens the throat so the air can get to the lungs more readily.) (Fig. 1)

4. Next, pinch the nose so the air won't leak back up and out. (Fig. 2)

5. Seal your mouth tightly around the victim's mouth and blow air into the lungs. Blow fairly hard. Then turn your ear to the victim's mouth and listen to make certain the air is being released. Repeat the process approximately twelve times a minute or twenty times a minute for a small child. *Don't quit.* Even if it takes hours and hours for professional help to get to you—which it may very well take—stay with it until that professional help arrives. (Fig. 3 & Fig. 4)

(Note: if you can't get the mouth to clear, or if you can't hear the victim releasing air when you turn your head sideways, seal his mouth with your hand and blow down through the nose.)

Usually, drowning victims will throw up while you

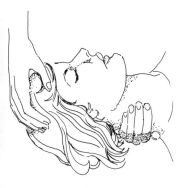

Fig. 1

Fig. 2

Fig. 3

Fig. 4

are giving first aid. Be ready for it and don't be squeamish. You cannot let it make you stop. Grab a rag, a piece of a shirt, or anything, wipe it up quickly, and clear the mouth once again. Watch your eyes while doing all this. The matter that is vomited is full of powerful acid and can do damage to your eyes if it hits them.

Remember to work through your squeamishness. If this situation does arise, it is a critical one. Mistakes can be life endangering, and whether or not *you* feel sick doesn't matter.

Chapter Seven

Equipment

At the top of the list of equipment needed for sailing is a *good* life jacket. Indeed, you don't truly *need* any other equipment (other than the boat, of course). You can sail without all the fancy tennis shoes and clothes that are sold. As a matter of fact, it's easier to sail without all that expensive junk that is pushed at you—sailing gloves, forty-dollar tennis shoes, ten-dollar wrist straps, expensive windbreakers—none of it is necessary.

But a life jacket is critical. Not only is it the first piece of equipment you should get, but you should thoroughly check it out before you get into a position where your life depends on it.

When I got my second sloop and we made ready to work the California coast, we bought a new kind of life jacket for my son. It was, apparently, Coast Guard approved, had all the stickers and labels on it, and said how much weight it would hold up.

The problem was that when my son put it on and got into the local swimming pool, he went to the bottom like a rock, labels, stickers and all.

So test the jacket or vest as soon as you get it and make certain it works.

Other special equipment needn't be expensive.

If at all possible, stay away from the specialized yachting supply stores and the like. You can have a lot of fun sailing without spending too much money, or you can have a lot of fun sailing and being broke all the time—the choice is yours.

The following is a list of some of the things you might find useful.

Tennis shoes. You don't need the expensive kind with all the little slits in the sole, although they're nice and they work. In fact, you can sail barefoot. But it always seems that your toe is slamming into something when you're barefoot, or you step out of the boat onto sharp rocks all the time.

A cap. Many people sail bareheaded, and of course a cap can sometimes blow off and be lost. But over the long haul, if you're going to sail all day, it's nice to have a baseball-type cap, just a cheap one, to keep the sun off the top of your eyes. It also helps you see things to have some shade over the top.

A waterproof pullover or zip-up windbreaker with a little hood. In sailing you are completely dependent on the weather, and that weather can do anything it wants. It always blows spray up on you, it seems, and the spray can be a bit cold, but more, it catches you in the rain. I can't count the number of times I've been sailing in lakes and gotten suddenly becalmed, only to get rained

SAILING: *From Jibs to Jibing*

on. A little windbreaker pullover, the kind that goes into its own pouch, can be awfully nice when it starts to rain or when the cool of the evening makes that bow spray start to cool down.

And that's about it. A small coffee can or plastic container for bailing is good to take along. Sailing is by definition a wettish sport and you might want a way to get rid of the water. Some people tie a small, cheap sponge on a string so it sits on the deck and every once in awhile give it a squeeze over the side.

Any other equipment is really unnecessary, and some of it can produce the opposite effect of what is wanted. Sailing gloves are supposed to protect the hands from rope burns, for instance, but in a way they keep the hands soft so they can't protect themselves. Without gloves, the ropes, wind, and water quickly toughen the hands—usually in two days—and after that you don't need the gloves. If you're using gloves and get in some good wind and then lose a glove—when the sail is pulling good and hard on your hands—you can come up with some fairly tender and bruised hands. Special sailing sunglasses, if you're used to wearing sunglasses, cost a fortune. Regular sunglasses do just as well. An elastic strap to hold the glasses on, especially prescription glasses, is a good idea.

All you need to sail is you, a life jacket, and a sailboat.

And some water.

And some wind.

Everything else is secondary.

Chapter Eight

First Attempts;
Meeting the Boat

Nobody ever forgets the first time he or she goes sailing. And it's usually for the same reason—it's a calculated, awe-inspiring, humbling disaster. One that leaves you shaking your head in wonder at how they *ever* got those big sailing ships to work.

In my own case a master sailor, a woman named Ruth, took me down to the dock and showed me the boat I would be learning in—a tiny, flat, water-soaked catboat with a heavy wooden mast and heavy canvas sails that made her so top-heavy she'd go over if you puffed on the sail. The whole affair was only 8 feet long, 2 feet wide, and six *inches* high on the hull. There was a daggerboard and a kind of hole for a cockpit and out in front of us a huge lake.

"That's it?" I asked. "We're going out in that?"

"Not quite right," she said. "*You* are going out in it. I'm not that crazy."

The gory details are probably boring so I won't go

into them except to say that I capsized *at* the dock, while still tied up. Capsized 4 feet from the dock, 8 feet from the dock, 20 feet from the dock, 40 feet from the dock, 60 feet from the dock—all to uproarious laughter from Ruth, bent over on the dock.

"You should try it when there's wind," she yelled. "Then it's *really* hard to keep up."

In that whole first day the longest run I made was on the order of 60 yards—and when I finally got that far I felt as if I'd conquered Mt. Everest. I have never—sailing small boats and large boats on lakes, rivers, and oceans—encountered a boat that viciously tender.

But—and this is an important but—when I finally, after days, got her to hold the wind and run, I knew much more than I would have known sailing some placid tub. Indeed, I had a wary feeling for the wind and its power that I still feel. I can't get in any sailboat without remembering that first savage little machine that taught me so much.

When you first come down to the boat sitting in the water, I would strongly urge you to try to get something a little saner than what I first had, but not something that doesn't move at all. Judging this difference in boats is easier than it might sound.

Sit towards the edge of the boat and see how tender it is. If the boat rocks quickly over to a point (all this while still tied at the dock, of course) and then stops before going on over, it's about right. If it goes on over and you get wet you might want to try a stiffer boat for your first venture. If it doesn't rock at all and just sits like a cow, it will take a half gale to get her moving and you might want to find something a bit lighter.

In any event, once you find a boat, you'll have to rig her out before you sail—get the sails up on her and the rudder on, if it hasn't already been done. All this is done on rentals and the boat sits ready to sail, but if you aren't renting you'll probably have to do it yourself.

The following is a quick rig-out section for those facing it for the first time.

The boat should be tied fore and aft to the dock, not so tight that it isn't floating, but not loose enough to wander around, either. Leave a couple of feet of slack on each rope.

With the boat tied securely, the first thing you do is drop the centerboard or put the daggerboard in and down. This is simple and straightforward. If the boat is large enough to have a let-down centerboard, there will be some kind of handle or crank on the centerboard housing in the middle of the boat. Simply release and crank the board down, all the way down. If it's a center daggerboard type, just slide it down into the slot and lock it in—if there's a lock on the housing. Sometimes there is a little thumbscrew to hold it in place.

With the board down in place there will be a bit of stability for you while you do the rest.

Next is the rudder. On the stern there will be two hinge-pin holes. On the rudder there will be two pins that fit into these holes, just drop the rudder so the pins

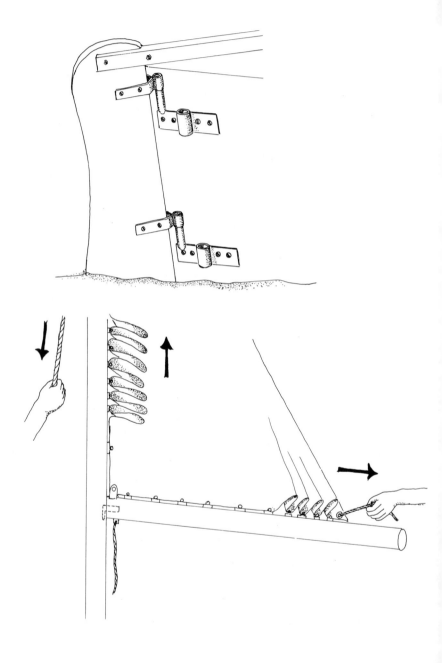

go into the holes. There will also be a small cotter-type pin or something that looks like a safety pin that goes through one or both of the rudder pins to keep it from popping back up out of place. Put this in or you'll inevitably lose the rudder at the most embarrassing moment.

With the rudder and the keel (or daggerboard or centerboard) in, the boat hull is done. Next, step the mast, which is simply done by putting the foot of the mast into the mast-mounting hole, somewhere just forward of the center of the boat. If there is any doubt about which end of the mast is the foot, or bottom, there will be a small bit of fastening hardware for the boom close to the bottom end of the mast. This is called the *gooseneck*.

When the mast is in, next comes the boom. Hook the hardware together at the gooseneck, where the boom attaches to the mast. They almost all have different kinds of fastenings, but they're easy to figure out and quick to do. For the moment just let the loose end of the boom lie across the back seat of the boat.

Consider the mainsheet next. This will be a long rope that is attached to the boom or the boat and goes up through a pulley arrangement on the boom or the boat (different boats put the pulley on the boom or in the boat or both).

The whole idea of all the pulleys and loops of rope is to give you more leverage and control of the sail. It is necessary to thread the rope correctly through the pulley

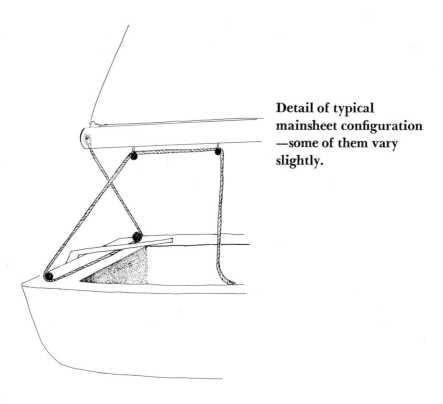

Detail of typical mainsheet configuration —some of them vary slightly.

on the boom and back down through the pulley on the boat. One end of the rope (sheet) is then left loose and the other end is affixed with a little eyelet to the proper place on the boat, either the boom, or on the boat itself, or on a sliding bracket on the stern of the boat. It all sounds confusing and is, but if you study the accompanying illustrations you'll find a way to do it right for the boat you're going to sail.

If all else fails, ask somebody for help. Tell the person you're just starting out and need a hand. Sailors love to give advice and help new people get started.

Now look at the sail, remembering that you are the master and it is just a piece of cloth. (The first time I

74

rigged out my own boat I did *not* remember that I was the master and that it was just a piece of cloth, and in moments I was reduced to frustrated rage.)

What I finally had to do to avoid confusion was find a large open area and lay the sail flat out on the ground. It will be a large triangular shape, with one arm of the triangle more pointed than the other. This long, pointed part is the top of the sail. The shorter pointed part is the part of the sail that goes out onto the boom and the square, or right angle corner of the sail is the foot, or the part that attaches where the boom joins the mast.

You will note that some provision for the sail to attach to the boom and mast will be on the sail. There will either be a series of little clips that slide on a rail on the mast and boom or there will be a rope sewn into the entire edge of the sail, which will fit into a tube sort of arrangement on the mast and boom.

Pick the sail off the ground by the top end and the outer end of the part that goes along the boom and carry it down to the boat. There, still holding onto those two ends, let the rest of the sail flop into the bottom of the boat where you can *gently* hold it down with your foot if the wind should gust suddenly and try to take it over the side.

First, slide the boom end of the sail out along the boom in whatever slide arrangement it has. Then take the head of the sail, the top, and start it in the groove or slide, which goes up along the mast. When it is up a foot or so, stop.

There will be a rope (*halyard*) for pulling the sail up as you go and there will be some ring or slip or hole at the top of the sail for attaching the halyard.

Attach the halyard to the sail and pull the sail up as you guide it into the groove or onto the little mast rail with the other hand. It sounds tricky but it's really very easy.

If there is any wind at all, as soon as the sail is up, or partially up, you will notice things come alive.

The wind will take the sail and it will quickly fill and blow over to the point where it is aimed up into the wind, and then it will start slamming and luffing back and forth.

Don't let it worry you. It's all normal; you just keep working the sail up the mast until it's almost to the top and then tie the halyard off on a cleat for the moment.

Now look once more at the foot of the sail, where it meets the mast and the boom. There will be a ring or hole or attaching device there, and it will go into an appropriate fastening device on the boom near the gooseneck area. It is a way to fasten the foot of the sail down and now is the time to do it.

On the outer end of the boom there will be a rope for pulling the sail out—it's called the outhaul—and making the bottom edge tight and stiff. Put the rope through the hole and grommet in the sail, pull it out as tight as you can, and tie it off to the cleat on the bottom or side of the boom.

Now pull the sail the rest of the way up the mast and tie the halyard off to a cleat on the side of the mast.

There's one more step. On most boats there will be a short rope at the bottom of the mast for pulling the boom down to make the vertical edge of the sail stiff and tight. This is called the downhaul, and this is the right time to pull it down—hard—and tie it off to the cleat on the opposite side from the halyard cleat. (The two tie-downs are interchangable and it doesn't matter which rope goes where, just so they don't both go to the same one.)

And *now* you're ready to sail.

Well, almost.

Put your bailing can or sponge in the boat, recheck your life jacket, make sure your shoes are tied and everything else is just perfect.

And *now* you're ready to sail.

One more piece of equipment that isn't really necessary but can prove a great help when you need it is an old canoe paddle. It can get you out of a rough place or two, and you can use it for fending off objects. Sometimes when you are becalmed a paddle will allow you to move the boat to light air places and get you home a bit sooner.

If you have a paddle put it in the boat under a seat.

And *now* you're ready to sail.

Getting the equipment together and ready to go is 90 percent of the work. The rest of it is all fun.

Before actually sailing sit in the boat at the dock for a few minutes and get the feel and reach of things. Let the sound work around you so you know each clink and luff, each movement.

Then untie the back rope and let her swing, still tied at the dock, to the wind. Note that a sailboat, under no control at all, sails up until it points dead into the wind and then hangs there, nose in the wind and waves. It's called "being in irons" if you're sailing. The boat just stops and everything luffs.

When you first start to sail, if something starts to go wrong or you feel that you're losing control of the situation, *let go of everything*. Let go of all sheets, turn the rudder loose, duck your head under the boom, put your hands in your lap, and just wait.

The boat will swing up into the wind, then slightly through, then back a lesser amount until it finally comes to rest nose into the wind with the sail and boom luffing and rattling and the sheets whipping around a bit. All of this will give you time to think about what you were doing wrong. Later we'll cover how to get out of irons and under way again.

For now, still tied at the rock, go over everything once again. Really *look* at things. Note how the wind works on the sail, feel how she moves with the wind, how the mast and sail move and that makes the hull move.

One of the primary moments of panic for many people who are just learning to sail is the movement and tipping action of the boat when it takes the wind. They forget

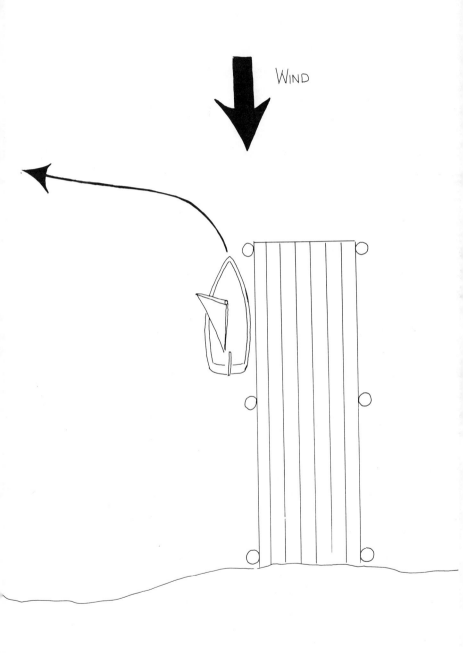

WIND

that it is *supposed* to tip and move, that's how it sails. It helps if, while sitting at the dock, you let the wind hit the sail a bit, perhaps even tighten the mainsheet a little and let the wind start to fill the sail so it will drive the boat over slightly and you can feel all the relationships involved. All the power of the wind on the sail comes down the mast into its foot, into the boat, and it is this movement of power, this relationship of sail to mast to boat to wind to you, that is most important in learning to sail.

Still at the dock, with the bow tied on a loose line—it is let out now to 6 or 8 feet and tied to the outer end of the dock—pull the sheets in tight and try moving the rudder back and forth to see how it works against the water and how it swings the stern back and forth opposite to its movement.

Pull it over hard a few times, hard and fast, and it will jerk the stern over enough to take the boat out of irons and the sail will fill. For a moment it will "sail" while tied to the dock, move forward a bit, then pull up on the rope. Do this maneuver a few times and part of what sailing is, how it works, will start to come to you.

Now push the rudder away hard a few times and get her to "sail" the other way. Do that several times to get a feel for the way the boat takes the wind and moves against the water and curves to the power of the wind.

It all might seem rather silly, sitting at the dock, pulling ropes and slamming the rudder back and forth. But learning the force of the wind and how it works on the

80

sail is vital, and there isn't a better way to get introduced to all of it than at the dock, where you can still control what happens.

When you are convinced that you know everything you can learn sitting at the dock it is time to get some water around you and get into basic maneuvers.

Or, as my wife rather wistfully and plaintively put it when she had never sailed before and I slipped the dock ropes and took our new boat out into the Pacific, "You mean we're really going out into the blue part?"

Slip that bowline loose and head out into the blue part.

Chapter Nine

Sailing, Moving on the Water

There is an old law in sailing—some call it the Forbes Law of Incorrect Wind—that states, simply put: "The wind is always in the wrong direction for you."

Of course, this is not strictly true. Many times I have had wind exactly as I wanted it and it took me just where I wanted to go. Still . . .

The one truly difficult way to leave a dock with a sailboat is when the wind is pushing the boat into the dock and against or towards the shore.

If you're lucky the wind will be the right direction to carry you on your way. But if Forbes Law comes into effect the very first time you go sailing, you will probably be looking right down the throat of a wind that's got the boat mashed into the dock or against the shore.

For that reason, before going into maneuvers in open water, we'll cover leaving the dock in a headwind. Which might also be called the anti-Forbes maneuver.

TACKING FROM THE DOCK

In truth it's that simple. When the wind is blowing onto the dock, the way to leave it is to tack upwind. You just align the boat off at an angle to the wind direction, trying to get as much outward as you can, pull the sheet in snugly, hold the rudder over so it won't let the boat nose up into the wind and you'll be moving.

If there's a wind the boat will heel over—you'll be on the high side so your weight will counterbalance the heeling action—and on your very first sail you'll get many of the initial joys of sailing. Beating to windward (going upwind), heeling, and, perhaps, getting dunked.

There's a little problem with just starting off on a tack from the dock. You can go left or right—as illustrated—and still get where you want to go, which is out in the body of water you're going to sail on, but there is a little snag.

No boat likes to start from dead stop and just move into an instant tack. There are too many forces acting against it—it's dead in the water, there's no curve of power developed on the sail and down through the boat, it's all static. To go right into beating to windward is against the nature of a still boat and if you try it the boat will probably just nose up into irons and you'll sit.

Instead, you've got to coax the boat into sailing, you've got to make the boat *want* to move upwind for you.

83

Actually you've just got to get some forward motion to the boat so it will answer the helm and turn to the rudder, but the business of coaxing is the old-fashioned way of putting it and sounds so much nicer. This coaxing is simply done. Aim the bow of the boat approximately 45 degrees off the wind, out at an angle, then nudge it forward from the dock or off the beach and steer off the wind a bit more yet, so the boat is leaving a tack and moving across the wind. The sail will fill immediately and the boat will start moving across the wind. As soon as it's moving well—inside 20 or 30 feet—tighten the sheets in and steer the boat back up into the wind to the correct tacking angle or the direction you want to go.

It's like a little curve just before you start moving. Later, after you know the boat, you'll be able to shorten this to the point where it will only take a few feet to get the boat going. As a matter of fact, anybody watching would think that you're just sailing the boat off the dock upwind.

All other ways off the dock are in a sense self-explanatory. You can reach or go downwind right from the dock, no coaxing necessary. Just perform the appropriate maneuver right off the dock and, presto, you're sailing.

The following are the basic maneuvers you will need to know to get started sailing. There are no embellishments, no fine-tuning concepts—they come a bit later. These are meant as an introduction only, and while great to do will only be by way of getting you started and having fun. Where you ultimately go with it depends of course on you.

GETTING OUT OF IRONS

Get out into the middle of the area you're going to use for sailing your first time—not way out, but out far enough so the wind isn't fluky from the bank—and then let everything go.

What we're trying to do is put the boat in irons, get it dead in the water. Later this will happen on its own, as you try the different sailing maneuvers, so it's good to learn about it at the start and know how to get out of it.

Get out into open water—even if you have to paddle or ride down the wind in a loose manner—and let everything go. You'll find the boat will rapidly swing around, perhaps oscillate a couple of times, and then come to rest with her nose up into the wind with the sail luffing and the boom rattling back and forth. If there's a lot of wind there will be a lot of noise, but it doesn't mean anything.

The boat is now in irons, effectively sitting still in the water, the wind doing no productive work on the sails. There *is* a tiny bit of movement: the boat will move backwards faintly as the wind pushes against the nose, but it's almost nothing.

The way to get out of irons is to use that faint back-

85

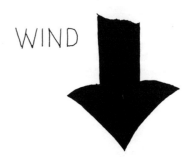

WIND

Backing out of irons.

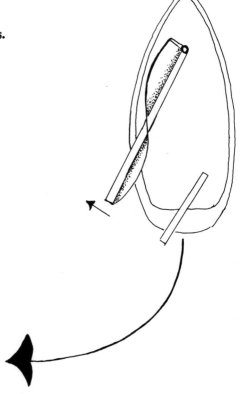

ward motion as a guide and capitalize and improve on it so that the boat will steer.

Reach up and hold the boom out to the side as far as you can with one hand. With the other one push or pull the rudder over to the same side as far as it will go.

What you're doing is physically forcing the bottom of the sail out into the wind so it will catch and develop a little power. It won't be much, but some, and it will be enough to start the boat moving backwards. First ever so slightly, then a bit more. If the wind is faint it might take some time. As the boat moves it will naturally answer to the rudder, which you have pushed over to the side.

It will steer backwards and around neatly until the wind is blowing across the boat instead of from the nose. As you remember from the clock graph earlier in the book, having the wind blowing across the boat is the ideal way to sail.

You rapidly pull the rudder all the way over to the *other* side of the boat, tighten the mainsheet (it's called "sheeting in") until the sail fills and has force, give it a few seconds, and you're off on a beam reach.

Don't stop with just one. As soon as you get out and under way, let everything go and let her swing back up into irons and do it again. Do it several times, until you know the boat and thoroughly understand what is happening when you go into irons. If you practice this maneuver for a time, it's amazing what you can learn about the response time of the boat, the way she answers to the helm, the quickness of her movement.

You'll also find getting out of irons to be a handy maneuver in other ways. Sometimes the wind will be right across a slip opening or other narrow slot so that the only effective way to sail the boat out is to sail it out backwards, just like getting out of irons. In that case you push the boom out, keep the rudder straight and let it sail straight back until you get where you want to be. Then push the tiller over, let her come around, take the wind across the beam, and sail out on a reach.

It's a very satisfying maneuver because getting in irons is so frustrating. It usually hits when the air is light and fluky and it's amazing to watch the number of people trying to paddle a boat around or scull it around with the rudder when all they have to do is hold the boom out and let the wind do the work.

Repeat it until you not only know the maneuver, but know the boat as well. It is a grand introduction.

BEAM REACH

As you come out of irons you go into a beam reach, the fastest way to sail and probably also the most fun. Here the wind is blowing straight across the boat from one side to the other, and the sail is sheeted in tightly, developing a great curve of power down into the boat, and you hold the rudder the opposite way from the boom, slightly, and the boat just creams along.

There is a great tendency when sailing on a beam reach to just forget the world and let her go until you run into a shore somewhere and have to stop. This is true especially if the wind is stout and steady. You can literally almost feel the boat come alive under your hand on the tiller, as the vibration of speed comes up through the rudder and centerboard. Often a boat moving fast on a beam reach will actually hum.

But before you forget the world and just take off, examine the whole idea of the beam reach and learn from it.

First, this is your initial experience with the tipping of the boat, the heeling. If the wind is fairly strong you'll note that the boat might heel over quite a lot and that you will actually have to lean out on the high side to keep her from going over.

This is called *hiking* and is part of the fun of a beam reach, or beating to windward. You use the mainsheet as a way to hang on, lean back out over the water, and you use your weight to try and make the boat come back up into the wind, to capture more force and go faster.

Along with heeling, the beam reach will also introduce you to the way the wind works on the sail. As you're sailing along on the reach let out some of the mainsheet and let the boom go out.

Let it all the way out. You'll see that as the sheet goes loose you lose the power of the wind and the sail goes out to the side where it hangs, luffing and not working.

Now start bringing the boom back in, pulling in on the sheet a few inches at a time. You'll feel the sail start to develop power, still luffing at first, then more and more until it's full and bellied out to the side and driving all its energy down the mast into the boat and making it move well across the water. At this point you have the optimum sailing condition.

Now keep sheeting in. Come in tighter still, *past* the optimum point but without moving the rudder from where it was best. This will make the boat heel more; a lot of people like to sail this way because it's more dramatic, but you will also note that the boat slows down.

As you come in tighter and tighter on the mainsheet, in past the best sailing point, the boat will heel more and more but continue to go slower and slower.

It will, eventually, stop. On large boats it will just hang there, over on its side with the wind holding it down, still in the water. It's called *blow-down*.

On smaller boats you can capsize this way, if you hold it too long and heel too far over. By coming close a few times on a beam reach, holding it until it comes over so the sail is just above the water and you're hardly moving forward at all, you have a really good way to learn more about your boat.

Sheet in a few inches at a time, feel her come through her power curve, then more until you get over on the side a bit and you'll know just where you can go before capsizing; know just how far you can go before you have to let everything go, put your hands in your lap, and let the boat come back up on its own.

Work at this for as long as the beam reach continues. Then get ready for the next maneuver. (We'll cover more of beam reaching later in the section on fine tuning your sailing.)

COMING ABOUT

No matter where you're sailing, even on the ocean, sooner or later you're going to have to turn the boat around and go the other way. It's called *coming about* and is one of the easiest things to do in sailing because it all more or less takes care of itself and happens automatically.

You're on a beam reach, coming close to the point where you'll have to turn. If there are passengers in the boat you will have to warn them of what you are going to do because the boom will move across the boat as you come about and they'll want to duck. The proper warning is "Ready about," but anything will work.

When you reach the turning point just let everything go.

The boat will swing around to put her nose into the wind immediately, bringing the boom across the center of the boat (as you and any passengers duck). Quickly grab the tiller and push it all the way in the opposite direction, bringing the nose of the boat on through the

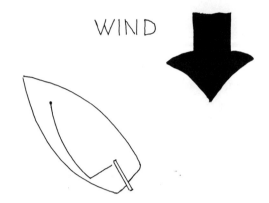

WIND

Coming about.

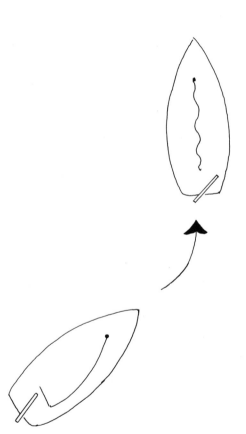

wind so that it's aimed in the opposite direction from the way you had been going.

Move quickly to the other side of the boat—the high side has now switched—pull in the sheet, tighten the sail into the power curve, pull the rudder over a bit to keep her on course, and you've done it, you've come about. You're on a beam reach going in exactly the opposite direction from the way you were going. (Reread the section on beam reaching and experiment the same way in the opposite direction to help you know the boat.)

The whole thing with coming about is that it's easy and quick to do as long as you keep your head down below the swing of the boom. Many people make it sound difficult but it's a natural function of sailing. When you let go, half the maneuver is done for you automatically; all you have to do is aid what's going on.

Practice coming about a few times to know the turning radius of your boat. The action, when you get it right and do it fast, will be kind of a round, swooping movement that will carry the boat around so fast it almost seems to turn within its own length. Indeed, you can turn a quick boat in its own length and be moving on a beam reach in the opposite direction almost before you know it.

On your first day of sailing, if you have good wind and open water, just go back and forth on beam reaches all day, practicing coming about on each end.

Work with the sails and the rudder and all the various

positions and combinations of each that you can possibly envision.

It is on the beam and broad reach where you get the most magnified expression of the relationship of wind, water, and the boat. The boat is moving at its fastest, it steers the "quickest," and the wind is blowing on the sail in the most powerful manner. It is, in short, the best of all circumstances to learn about sailing and about your boat, or the boat you are using.

Try sheeting out (letting the mainsheet out a little at a time) as you are sailing along. The boat quickly loses speed, comes up off the heel, and gets sloppy in the water. When you sheet back in, the boat will "quicken" and go faster and seem more alive.

That feeling, that quickening, is what you're looking for, regardless of the form of maneuver you are doing. Up or down wind, or across the wind, that coming alive of the boat is the whole concept of sailing and happens if you're sailing a dinghy or a clipper ship.

So go back and forth on the beam reach until you know and feel as much as you can about it. This can't be stressed too much. The beam reach is where all the theory comes into practical use. It shows you how the sheets work with the rudder, how different heeling angles affect speed (more on that later in fine tuning), how speed affects turning when you come about. As one man who taught me sailing said: "The beam reach is a sailing course in itself."

So stay with it.

BROAD REACH

For many people of the old sailing school, a broad reach is what sailing is all about. It is sailing when the wind truly drives the boat through the water and, while not necessarily the fastest (beam can be faster), it is somehow the most powerful way to sail.

In the old sailing days, when the tall ships, the mighty clippers, moved on the oceans, the broad reach was what they looked for, what they lived to find. Sometimes they would go three or four hundred miles out of their way to find such a wind, to get "on the reach."

This is when the wind not only comes from the side, but slightly from the rear as well.

If you are on a beam reach and want to go to a broad reach you merely sheet out a few inches, maybe a foot, and turn the rudder so that the boat moves off the wind, moves a bit more away from the wind than it had been on the beam reach.

That's a broad reach.

You will note that the boat immediately loses a bit of speed, loses most of the heeling action, but seems to drive with more purpose through the water; it moves with a kind of authority.

Many people feel that the broad reach is the most comfortable way to sail because the boat is more level and yet still moves well, and that may be. If you are sail-

ing a heavy boat—what's called a "hog" in sailing circles
—you will find that it moves better on a broad reach
than it did on the beam reach. That's because more of
the power of the wind is taken directly into the sail and
down the mast. This is the reason the old clipper ships
worked so hard to get a broad reach. They were im-
mensely heavy and needed the extra power to move their
weight, whereas something light and quick—like a small
sailing catamaran—does better on a beam reach where it
can get up on one side hull and not have to drive weight
through water but skim over the top.

It's a good thing to remember if you have weight in
the boat—a couple of passengers or camping gear if
you're going on a sailing trip. You might want to get in
a position where a broad reach will work for you rather
than settle for a beam reach, it actually might be faster.

In sailing, the shortest distance between two points—
at least when considering time involved—is most de-
cidedly *not* a straight line. It is where the wind will work
for your boat and your particular situation the best. If
you are heavy in the water, in the long run a broad reach
will prove to be faster than a beam reach.

As with the beam reach, work the broad reach back
and forth for an entire day, or until you're comfortable
with your knowledge of the maneuver.

Practice going from a beam reach over to a broad
reach, a maneuver rather romantically called "falling off
the wind."

When you reach the end of a broad reach run, you

come about in exactly the same way as you did with the beam reach. Let her nose come up into the wind, help her on through the wind with the rudder, move to the other side of the boat as you do all this, sheet in on the other side, and off you go.

Moving from beam to broad reach is important, because falling off the wind is the first step in going to the most difficult part of sailing, if it can be called difficult—sailing downwind.

So work at it, practice it until all of it is automatic. Stay with it until the beam reach, the broad reach, and coming about are things you can do without thinking. In the next chapter we'll cover sailing downwind, and you'll need to know the reaching maneuvers before moving with the wind.

A word or two on steering.

As you practice reaching it is a good time to start work on your steering procedures and this is a little more complicated than just making the boat go left and right.

First, work at steering to the wind. Set the mainsheet where you want it, then leave it there and move the boat back and forth with the rudder.

You will find that the rudder has much more control over the boat than the wind, though it is much smaller in area. This, of course, is because water is so much denser than air.

Use the rudder to steer upwind and slightly downwind, not too far downwind because you might hit the uncontrolled jibe area, which can have disastrous results. Learn how the boat feels as it takes the wind correctly, using only the rudder for control—that's part of steering.

The other part is getting where you want to go. It's all well and good to just hit for the middle of the lake and sail back and forth for awhile, but what if you want to go somewhere?

As you practice reaching, start to practice steering for a particular point. Aim at something on the shore and make for it, or try to.

You will find that though the wind isn't blowing properly for you to make a beam or broad reach right to where you want to sail, you can juggle things around until you get the direction you want. By sheeting out a bit, working the rudder a bit, you can make the boat sail the direction you want to go. Maybe not as fast, maybe not with as much purpose. But if there is a wind you will be able to get the boat to go exactly where you want it to go.

What's more, you will be able to do this without any noise, without any fumes, without any use of any non-renewable resource whatsoever. Just by tapping the power of the wind, sticking your sail up and borrowing a little force from the wind.

So why did they invent outboards?

Chapter Ten

Sailing Downwind

For me, sailing downwind has always been the most uncomfortable way to sail, especially if you are on a body of water large enough to have even moderate waves.

When you turn a boat downwind it loses all side-push, all heeling motion, and all roll stability; as the waves come from the rear and go under the boat they set up a peculiar rolling motion that can be uncomfortable. Significantly, it is while moving downwind—either under power or sail—that most people get seasick.

For that reason, when I'm sailing I try to avoid the downwind condition. I'll go further out and come back on a very broad reach and avoid the whole downwind run.

Despite its possible discomfort, however, it is a very beautiful way to sail and is worth doing just for the beauty of it. In a late-afternoon sun, right when it's going into gold evening, running before the wind with the gold light up on the sail is like moving through a wonderful dream.

Then, too, there will come that rare time when you

have to sail downwind to get where you want to go, even if it's just for a short space to get into a dock.

So downwind sailing is something you need to know and know well, as well as any other part of sailing.

What happens in downwind sailing is quite simple. You fall farther and farther off a broad reach, sheeting out more and more until the boom is straight out to the side. Then you hold the sheet to keep it from going out anymore and steer straight downwind with the wind at your back.

The sail can be out to either side and the whole maneuver is easy to accomplish, easy to start.

What can be hard about downwind sailing is making sure the wind is straight from your back. As you turn and start to go downwind, you begin to move in the same direction as the wind, and if there's any possible wave action, you rapidly lose all sensation of movement. Since you're moving with everything, there are no indications of wind direction, or at least they aren't as pronounced as they are in other sailing positions.

As a matter of fact, you can be in a fairly stout wind and feel as if you're in a dead calm when you turn downwind.

For this reason steering downwind is harder to do than in other maneuvers. There is a tendency to wallow around a bit and move off at one angle or another, and this causes a secondary problem that can be disastrous.

You may get too loose with your steering while running before the wind, forget the wind direction for a

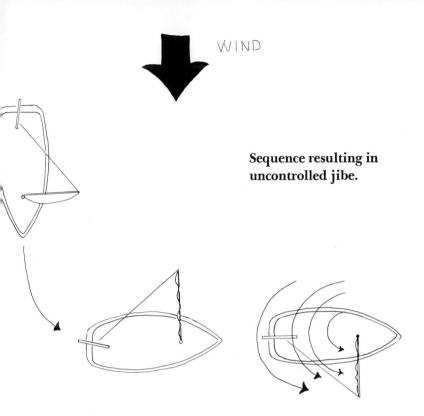

WIND

Sequence resulting in uncontrolled jibe.

time and steer so far around that the boom is pointing back upwind. Then, the wind can get on the *other* side of the sail and—without knowing it's happening—you get what is called an uncontrolled jibe.

The sail will whip from one side of the boat to the other and the boom will go with it, whistling across like a fast freight train, taking down anything in the way. If you're not ready for it, the uncontrolled jibe can give your head a nasty crack. With larger boats it can be even worse. When the boom whips across it develops a tremendous amount of snap-power, and when it slams into the other side, all of that power concentrates where the boom meets the mast. There is so much power at that

101

point that it's possible for the mast to break and come down, just shatter and drop. This won't happen on small boats, but you can get a headache out of it and if there's a good wind and you go into an uncontrolled jibe it's possible that you'll capsize.

So as you steer downwind, be sure to keep the wind straight at your back. Luckily, there are some indications of wind direction you can use to keep yourself heading the right way.

No matter how fast the boat you are sailing may be, you will never truly match the speed of the wind. You might come close, but you won't match, so you will still feel a faint breeze on the back of your neck. If your boat has wind direction indicators (telltales), they will show a slight movement downwind. If not, you might carry a piece of yarn and hold it up now and then to check. It will blow out with the wind, hanging downwind slightly.

Also watch the water and any wave action there may be. While it isn't too accurate, it will furnish you with a general form of knowledge, which can be helpful. The waves will be moving a little faster than you, and they are moving with the wind, so if you watch them and run parallel to their movement you'll be all right.

Don't use something on shore to steer by. There's a desire to lock the nose of the boat on something on the shore, a tree or building, and just hold her rock steady to run before the wind. But wind has a habit of changing right when you least expect or want it to change. A sudden change in wind direction is the most common reason for an uncontrolled jibe. It can come around so fast without warning that you can go from normal downwind sailing to an uncontrolled jibe in seconds.

If you're steering to something on shore, and not steering to the wind, you can almost bet that you're going to have an uncontrolled jibe, at least when you're going downwind. This is true especially if you're sailing in a place with high cut banks around the shore, or in mountain lakes, where the wind is always unpredictable.

The real trick in sailing downwind and avoiding an uncontrolled jibe is to turn it into a controlled jibe.

It's easy to do, and it turns something like a tiger into something close to a kitten.

CONTROLLED JIBE

Put the boat into a broad-reach condition, then keep going until you are aiming straight downwind, sheeting out more and more until you are sailing downwind with the boom out to the side.

Now *keep* turning in the same direction, so that you go past the straight downwind condition and start off to the other side. This, of course, puts the boom closer and closer to pointing back up into the wind, setting up the conditions for an uncontrolled jibe.

As soon as you go past the downwind direction and into the area where you're approaching an uncontrolled

103

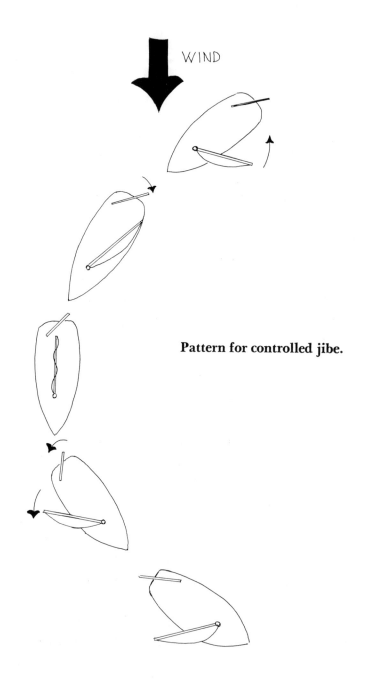

WIND

Pattern for controlled jibe.

jibe, begin sheeting in as you keep turning, pulling the boom back up into the jibe. In other words, you're going to make the jibe happen before it can come on its own and be uncontrollable.

Just keep pulling in on the sheet as you turn and the boom will come around against the wind more and more until it's pointed straight back upwind and, finally, through the eye of the wind and out the other side—all under control with your hands on the rope.

As the wind takes the other side of the sail and pushes it over—it will be a kind of rapid, swooshing motion—you begin letting the sheet out smoothly, until the boom is out to the side once again and you are sailing downwind, or actually, on a very broad reach.

All you're doing is flopping the sail from one side of the boat to the other, really, but doing it under a wind and sailing condition.

It is one of the paradoxes of sailing that while you hardly ever have to run straight down the wind, you quite often find yourself in a place where a jibe will save a lot of time and effort. Good examples are coming into dock, or weaving through crowded areas where there are a lot of boats, or avoiding snags or other obstacles. Somehow, the jibe always seems like a handy thing just when you expect it least.

For that reason it is strongly recommended that you practice the jibe as much as possible when you first start sailing. As with reaching, spend an entire day in good wind going from a reach on one side through a jibe and

SAILING: *From Jibs to Jibing*

out to a reach on the other. Then back again, falling off the wind to straight downwind, then through a controlled jibe, and out the other side on a reach.

It is the second way to turn the boat—after coming about with her nose up through the wind—and as such a very handy thing to be able to do well. Work at it until you can jibe as easily as coming about.

Once you are finished, spend another day or so reviewing all the techniques you've learned so far. Work on the lake or river or harbor until you've conquered all the reach positions, from beam down to broad, and through wing and wing and the controlled jibe.

When you have them all you will have attained the ability to steer a sailboat any where you want to go as long as it's in a downwind direction.

Now all that remains is sailing back upwind to get back to the dock.

Chapter Eleven

Sailing Upwind

Tacking upwind, sailing upwind, beating, beating to windward, hard slogging, hull slamming, wet sailing—there are many terms to describe it, but they all mean the same thing.

You are going to take a boat with a sail on it, a boat that you think will only sail *with* the wind, and you are going to make that boat sail back up *against* the direction of the wind.

It is a little hard to believe, even when you do it. Indeed, for many generations, sailing boats and ships couldn't sail up against the wind, couldn't "point very high," as it's put. They just sat and waited until the wind changed to the direction they needed to get to their destination on a reach or run downwind.

Nobody knows for sure when the concept of a long keel came into effect, but with it came the ability to sail upwind. With that keel or board sticking down in the water, the boat can't slide sideways across the water and some of the sideways push can be changed into forward motion.

SAILING: *From Jibs to Jibing*

It becomes possible to sail a boat against the wind that is driving it, at least to within 45 or so degrees of the wind —enough so that by going back and forth—tacking—it's possible to average the movement out so that in effect you wind up going straight back up against the wind. It takes longer to get from one point to the other, up to twice as long, but it can be done. For me it's always been one of the true marvels of sailing, almost a gift. A boat that moves with the wind, is pushed by the wind, can be made to go against the wind.

There are several theories as to why this works, but the most popular one is that the sail of the boat works somewhat like the wing of an airplane. As you nose up into the wind on your tack, the wind that goes around the outside of the sail, out around the belly of the sail, has to move further and at a greater speed than the wind that cuts across the inside of the sail. This, most authorities agree, establishes pull, or "lift," in a forward direction the way air forced to go over the top of an airplane wing establishes lift in an upward direction. However it works, it gets the job done and it is also easy to do.

From a beam reach, sailing across the wind, you just turn the bow up into the wind and sheet in the sail. The more you turn up into the wind, the more you sheet in —the more you tighten the sail in relation to the wind.

If you try to point too high—too much up into the wind—the boat will just go into irons and hang there until you bring it back out and go back to a beam reach.

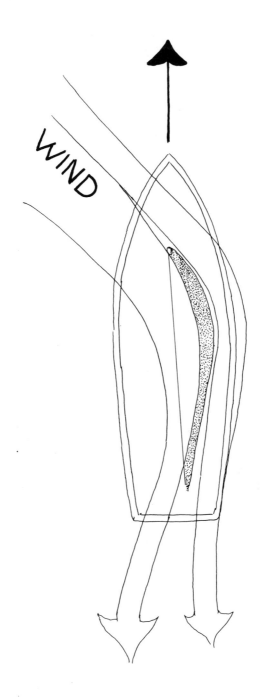

WIND

If you don't point high enough you don't go upwind and just run back and forth on a beam reach.

Since every boat is different and will point to a different angle in a different wind, you must find out where your boat points on your own. Just nose her up into the wind, tighten the sheet, and look for the best angle to the wind that you can get.

Some things you will notice are discussed here, which will help you know what to expect. First, you will find that going to windward, if there's any wind at all, can tend to be a bit damp. Since you're bucking any wave action there might be, the waves will slap against the bow, and since you're also bucking the wind, the resulting spray will blow back at you. It's all part of sailing and fun, especially on a hot summer afternoon when the spray can cool you down. But it can be a bit startling if you aren't ready for it.

There is also much more authority to the wind— even a mild wind—when you're beating up against it. Since you're going against it, it seems stronger and heels the boat with more force, if not harder and further. There's never any danger or difficulty. Just be ready for taking it in the face, taking it with more power, and there won't be any trouble.

One of the greatest surprises I ever had sailing was the first time I took out my first cruising sloop. It was a gorgeous Pacific afternoon, the sea a slate blue with moderate waves, and a 12- to 15-knot wind. Just perfect.

I turned out of the harbor entrance and ran south with the wind, on a broad reach, for 7 or 8 miles—sipping tea, steering with my foot, watching the dolphins around the boat.

Then I turned to come home.

I was stunned to find myself going against waves that seemed huge, that slammed like giant hammers into my hull, that covered me constantly with spray and shook everything down inside that was loose, opened drawers, slammed stuff around. The wind tore at me, the same wind that had been so peaceful but a moment ago.

I thought I had somehow come into a sudden squall, a wild little storm of wind. I fell off the wind again, turned back to the reach, and everything was as peaceful as before.

It was then, and on the ensuing beat home, that I realized when the oldtimers coined the phrase "beating to windward," they meant exactly what they said—it's a beating.

In small boats nothing that dramatic will probably ever happen. But you will get wet, count on it.

Remember to reckon with the time element. Tacking up against the wind and going back and forth to get where you want to go can be time-consuming. The wind and water both have a tendency to push you back as you try to move forward, and the end result is that you get pushed back and down a bit.

If you're on a critical schedule and you have to be

back at a certain time, be cautious about running too far downwind so you'll have to tack back up.

An hour's fun across a lake with the wind can be a good four hours of wet slamming to get back. If you're in a hurry to get home, better start by going upwind and then run back before the wind later.

Chapter Twelve

Using Two Sails

You now have all the basic skills and knowledge to sail. You can take a small boat anywhere you want to go, as long as there's wind.

Small sailboats are amazingly agile and responsive, and as you practice and sail more and more, you'll find there is almost nothing you can't do with one. In fact, in a later chapter we'll discuss secondary uses of small sailboats, where you don't just go out and sail around but actually use them for a secondary purpose—sailing-camping, sailing-hiking, fishing. They are truly versatile craft and can open up whole new worlds of use for you if you work with them a bit.

For the moment, review all the maneuvers of sailing. For a good week of afternoons, if you can get the boat-time, go out and work with honing up your abilities. Practice all the maneuvers again and again, steer to imaginary points and then come back. Work at every possible maneuver combination you can possibly work at, going from one to the next as fast as you can and as fast as the boat will answer. Take the boat around, for instance, from a tack upwind on one side to a reach, down to running with the wind, through a controlled jibe, up through a reach on into a tack upwind on the other side—all in one maneuver.

Really work at practicing, at getting it burned into your mind so that all the maneuvers and combinations are automatic.

"You want to sail," my advanced teacher taught me, "as you would walk. Without thinking."

When you are at that stage, or getting to a point where nothing surprises you and you know the boat well, examine the concept of a second sail.

Most small sailboats—dinghies and skimmer-type boats —only have one sail. But as you move up a bit—still in small boats, but just above the really small ones—you get into an area where they are starting to incorporate a second sail into the design.

This sail goes in front of the mainsail, is a small triangular-shaped sail, and is called the jib. Or, if you'd rather, the foresail, front sail, nose sail, forward sail, turning sail, or fore rag, depending on who is talking.

For our purposes it will remain the jib.

If you should move up into a boat large enough to have a jib, you will find that it goes faster, points a bit higher to the wind, turns a bit faster, and is a little more controllable.

As for sailing it, it is exactly the same except that you must contend with another sail—a pulling sail to match

Typical two-sail small boat showing jib in place.

the push of the main—and an extra set of two sheets to control the jib sail. It's a bit more complicated on turns, but once you've mastered sailing with a single sail you can pick up using a jib in a couple of hours or even less out on the water.

First, it rigs out more easily than the mainsail. Shackle the foot of the sail to the nose of the boat in the appropriate latch (they're all different but easy to figure out), and put all the hooks around the cable that runs up to the top of the mast (it's called a stay). There will be another halyard, which you hook into the top of the jib to pull it to the top of the mast, or as far up as it will go. In general, a jib for a small boat doesn't go all the way to the top; it will be what's called a three-quarter rig rather than a full rig.

Next, lay the sheets out. There will be two of them, two long ropes coming off the loose end of the jib. One of them comes out around the mast to the left, the other to the right, and they are left to lie loose for the moment in the bottom of the cockpit or boat opening.

With the main and jib up you will notice more noise. The jib has a tendency to pop and crack even more than the main, so don't be alarmed when the noise increases dramatically. It's just the popping of the sail as it fills with wind and then suddenly releases it.

Sailing with the jib is the same as sailing without the jib. A beam reach is still across the wind, a broad reach is the same—the only thing that changes is running downwind, but more of that in a moment.

As you start out sailing in a boat with a jib, first pay attention to the main. For example, say that you are leaving the dock on a beam reach.

First you set the mainsail; tie it off to a cleat when it's drawing well and in its full power curve. This takes only a moment. Then, without changing steering or the main, you pull in on the downwind sheet of the jib and tighten it in until it conforms to the curve of the mainsail and is pulling well.

That's it.

When you want to come about and go on a beam reach in the other direction, you do it the same as if you didn't have a jib. Bring the boat up through the wind, without touching the mainsheet. The mainsail will take care of itself because it's tied off and you're going to just reverse everything. It will swing over and fill on the opposite side.

As the nose of the boat comes through the wind, release the jib sheet you've been holding and take up the jib sheet on the opposite side, sheeting in until the jib sail is full, curved, and conforming to the curve of the mainsail.

It all sounds a little complicated, and the first time you face dealing with the extra set of sheets and the extra sail flapping around can be a bit disconcerting. But after a couple of practice maneuvers you'll pick it up fast and then you'll wonder how you ever sailed without a jib.

Almost all the maneuvers are essentially the same. On beating to windward, tack to where you want—or can get—set the mainsail first and then set the jib to conform to the curve of the main on the downwind side. You will find on beating upwind that the jib will help considerably and enable you to point higher, so you might want to tune things up a bit after you first set all the sails. Tighten the mainsheet again, just a tad, and then tighten the jib up a bit to match it.

Some sailors work constantly at retuning the jib and main to get the best power curve out of the combination of the two sails, to get them to "draw" well through the slot between the sails. You should work at understanding how the two sails on your boat (they're all a little different) work together. But at first, set the main and get the jib to conform to the curve—that's a good rule.

The exception to the rule is sailing straight downwind. You start the same, heading the boat downwind and pushing the main way out to the side. Then you use the jib sheet to tease and kind of flip the jib out to the other side so that it fills out in front like a kind of pulling parachute. The sheet will have to be quite loose to accomplish this, and you'll have to work at it some to get the sail to fill and stay filled. At first it can be frustrating because the jib tends to want to pull ahead and flop back and try to hide from the wind in front of the main. But stay with it and you'll be rewarded with more speed, more power on the sail curve, and a gorgeous sight.

In a good wind with a clean sun there isn't anything quite as pretty as a boat being pulled wing and wing out across the water. It's somehow like the joy and line of a gull, swooping across the surface.

When you get comfortable with all the maneuvers and combinations of maneuvers and feel as if the jib is

118

WIND

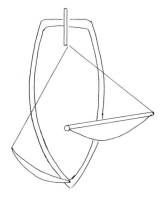

Wing and wing with jib sail in front.

part of your sailing knowledge, take the main down and tie the boom off to the side and practice sailing on the jib alone.

Whereas the main pushes, you'll soon find that the jib pulls, and in so doing it tends to raise the nose of the boat ever so slightly. This is good information to know, because when you're beating to windward, if you let the jib pull just a shade harder than the main it will raise the nose of the boat a bit and might keep you a bit drier.

The boat will sail much more slowly on the jib alone, of course, and will take longer to do all the maneuvers. It will not sail up into the wind—it has no pointing ability to speak of—but it will sail. Sailing the jib alone for a day can teach you a tremendous amount about your boat and your sailing ability. Give yourself plenty of sea room, get out in the middle somewhere, and take the main down and spend an afternoon on the jib. It will enhance your whole sailing experience.

The jib is a "tricky" sail, not in a bad way, but in a good one. There are many tricks which, if you know them, will make the jib one of your most useful sailing tools.

The idea of the jib holding up the front end of the boat slightly is one trick—it will keep you dry. But when used in conjunction with the mainsail, it will also turn the boat a lot faster. That's a nice thought to have in the back of your mind if you ever get into a tight spot where you need to come about in a hurry.

All you do is hold the jib sheet a little too long when you come about. Instead of letting go of the jib sheet on the high side as the nose goes through the wind, keep it tight for a moment. The jib will also go through the wind, and the sail will catch the wind on its back side. This will help to push the nose of the boat through the wind and out the other side quite fast. As soon as you feel the push start to take the nose around—and it will be a definite surge—let go of the sheet on the high side and take up the sheet on the other side. It can cut your turning time and margin by a great amount, and if you're caught in thick traffic or coming into rocks you didn't see, it's good to know you can whip that nose around a little faster and shorter.

Another useful trick with the jib is to use it in bad weather. You should never get caught out in truly bad weather in a small boat, but if something should nail you out of nowhere and the wind gets up, bring the boat's nose into irons and drop the main and tie it off. Then let it fall back off the wind until it fills the jib and run downwind to shore with only the jib flying.

Since it tends to pull the nose up a bit, you won't have quite so much trouble with hitting waves. Since the jib is smaller than the main it won't have anywhere near the same tendency to capsize the boat. Because the sail pulls instead of pushes it makes steering downwind in strong wind a lot easier; it gives the boat kind of a pulling-following feeling.

Finally, if you're caught in irons and have a jib, it's easier to get out. Go up and hold the jib out to the side by grabbing right where the sheets tie into the sail and holding that corner out. The wind will quickly "back" the jib and push the nose around so the main can fill with wind and you're on your way. It's a lot faster than using the main alone to get out of irons.

"The jib," one of my teachers used to say, "is like having an extra person on board. It'll do everything but bring you food."

Not quite. But it's a handy sail to have and one you can learn to like.

Chapter Thirteen

Care and Stowage of Equipment

In only one other outdoor endeavor in my experience has the proper care and use of equipment been as vital as it is in sailing. That's when I was working a dog team on a long line in the north country. Anything that goes bad through neglect or improper use can cause real trouble—and the dogs have a way of finding anything weak and making it come to the surface.

It is the same in sailing. Any shortcut, any quick attempts to go the easy way, any equipment that is run down or not repaired, any weak spot, any gear that is incorrectly stowed (put away), any sail that isn't tied off correctly—anything on that order tends to wait until the exact wrong moment and then jumps up and takes over the situation.

Take something really simple, like the mainsheet. Normally, as you sail, it will lie in the bottom of the boat in loose folds, ready to be let out or pulled in as need be, and that's as it should be. But if you get careless and let it wrap around your ankle once and don't pull your ankle out of the loop, you have the potential for a problem. The first time you do a controlled jibe and find that you have to let a lot of rope out as the sail fills suddenly, and then look down as the snake of a rope tightens around your ankle—ahh, that's one of the great moments of sailing. You get a distinctive rope burn around your ankle, the sail hangs up halfway around, a controlled jibe quickly becomes an uncontrolled jibe, and you stand a good chance of capsizing as the sail hangs up and drags the boat around, over, and down.

All because of one loop around your ankle.

Watch all of your gear all of the time, and if something is incorrect fix it at once. If you don't, the boat will show you why you should. The following are some guidelines on what to watch out for and how to remedy the problem.

WHILE SAILING

First, all ropes—sheets—should be loose and neatly folded so they'll feed out correctly and not around anything or under anything or through anything. All sheets should be free of any form of knot or potential knot or any kinks. If one of the sheets is kinked, work it back by uncoiling it as you go until the kink is worked out. A kink will rapidly turn into a knot just when you don't want or need it. Always coil the rope with a rope twist to avoid kinks. Also make certain that all the sheets—if

SAILING: *From Jibs to Jibing*

you're sailing with two sails—are kept separate. Sheets
are notorious for intermingling, and if left to themselves
on the floor of the boat they will quickly coil around
each other and become tangled. You haven't lived until
you go through an uncontrolled jib with your mainsheet
tangled with both your jib sheets. It's like having two
cobras in the boat with you while a tiger jumps on your
back.

Any loose gear—bailing cans, paddle, sponges, camping or fishing gear—should be lashed down out of the
way when not in actual use. There are two reasons for
this. First, and obviously, should the boat go over, you'll
lose it all and if the water is deep and the material doesn't
float it's gone. But more important, with loose gear the
idea of being cautious about it is always in the back of
your mind. When you do get in a tight spot and think
the boat might be going over, rather than sail out of
it or remember what to do, there's a tremendous urge
to try and save all the sinkable gear. When you're worry-
ing you can't sail right, so keep a tight boat with everything lashed down when not in use.

Finally, while sailing, keep studying your boat and
sails and rigging and gear. If something is loose, ragged,
ripped, or frayed make a mental note of it and fix it as
soon as you get done sailing. Some people we talked to
keep a small notebook and write down any discrepancies
they see as they go along, so they won't forget them when
they get back on shore.

Primarily, while sailing, watch those points where

there is movement or normal wear; the rudder hinge pins, or the little sliders that go up along the mast to attach the sail, the sheets where they go through blocks, the tiller where it attaches to the rudder, the centerboard housing. All of these are wear areas and should be watched. If you note any wear or loosening or rot, fix it as soon as you can.

If you have a wooden boat, look for dark spots that show the beginnings of rot. When you see such spots, sand them down as soon as you get a chance and use touch-up varnish or clear plastic coating to recover them. It amounts to continual touch-up, but it never takes very long and it will definitely save a lot of work later on— it may prevent the necessity of stripping and refinishing the whole wood surface or replacing a major piece of wood.

Watch the sails. They take the most wear and tear. With modern fabrics, rot is no longer a consideration, but they can still tear, rip, and puncture, so keep your eye on them—especially where there are any grommets —and fix them with the appropriate method if you see anything wrong.

WHILE AT THE DOCK

When you finish sailing it's time to perform any and all maintenance on the problems you saw while out on the water. Do them right away or as soon as you can.

Damage has a way of snowballing, and where one or two minor problems won't bother you much, a whole raft of them can ruin a sailing day.

When you get back, also look at those portions of the boat you couldn't see when you were out sailing. Check out the bottom of the boat: if it's wood, look for rot or cracks; if it's fiberglass look for major cracks or breaks. Next, study the rudder and the dagger or centerboard. These are items that stick down and they take a beating every time you come on rocks or get too close to shore.

Even a glass boat will probably have a wooden— maybe plywood—centerboard and rudder, so look for chewed wood or ripped and torn edges. When you see them, repair them—before you sail again—to make sure the water doesn't soak in and have time to start rotting the wood.

This is also the time to reexamine all your personal gear—life jacket, shoes, clothing—to make sure they are in good, or usable, shape. If something is wrong, either repair it, or, in the case of a damaged or ruined life jacket, replace it. Don't try to sail with bad or possibly weakened gear. It always seems to let you down.

All of this sounds pretty obvious, and perhaps it is, but it is also very important. One of the constant aspects of sailing is the maintenance. Sailing is hard on boats and hard on gear; there's a lot of power going into that sail, and a lot of good enjoyable use coming out.

Taking care of your gear is an important part of sailing.

The final aspect of the treatment of gear while using the boat is stowage of gear temporarily between uses. The classic example of this is if you're sailing-camping and wish to leave your boat tied up for the night, or if you're visiting somebody and want to leave the boat tied to a dock.

Take the sail down and kind of roll it up on top of the boom and tie it in three places to the boom with short straps or pieces of rope so that the wind won't tear it loose and fill it and start mucking things up when you aren't there.

When you're leaving the boat temporarily, all loose ropes should be neatly coiled. While it's true that this looks nice, the reason for doing it isn't only neatness. When you come back and get ready to sail everything will be ready to go, ready to feed out, which is nice. But if you're camping and you have to do something with the boat after dark, you'll know that the ropes aren't tangled, that you can depend on everything being where you need it. That can be critical.

Chapter Fourteen

Repair

"Generally speaking," an instructor told me, "sailboat repair can be broken down into three categories: the sail, the boat, and you." We'll cover the repair section in that order, working from the top down.

Before we get into specifics, there is one overall repair note that has to be brought to the fore.

When making repairs and when getting materials for repairing your boat or sails, if at all possible, stay away from marine hardware supply outlets or chandlers. There are some special items you might have to buy at those places, special shackles or blocks or rope, but for screws or materials stay away from them. With no exceptions in all the research we did over several years for the book, every single such outlet we checked or used was enormously overpriced. Sometimes this overpricing would be as low as 50 or 60 percent above normal—for the same item, same brand that could be purchased at a regular hardware store—but often it was *700* or *800* percent higher.

Even if you're rich, such overpricing is outrageous.

If you live close to the bone, like us, that extra money can be better spent in getting good-quality repair material at regular hardware or discount outlets and doing the job right.

SAIL REPAIR

There are many things that can—and usually do—go wrong with sails. We'll start with what we've found to be the most common repair problems and work into the rarest.

Loose stitching

Whether from the constant luffing they undergo or the rap-rapping of the wind even when they're being fully used, somehow the stitching always seems to come loose in sails. This happens primarily around the sticks that stiffen the edges, the battens, but it also comes in other areas, so keep your eyes open.

The repair, of course, is to resew the area that has come loose. There is a guideline in working on any boat repair that applies as a basic rule: in any repair, on any part of the boat, make the repair better and stronger than it was in the first place, better than new.

Get a roll of white nylon prewaxed thread, the heavy kind they use for shoe and boot repair. If they don't have it at the regular hardware store you can get a roll from some shoe repair shops. One roll will last you a lifetime. Then get a moderately large needle with an eye big enough to take the waxed thread. Some sailors keep a small pouch with this thread and a needle and a small pair of pliers tied up under a seat or up in the covered bow.

As for the sewing of the repair, there are several ways to go. You can redo the same kind of sewing that was there originally. This will hold about as well as the original stitching, which was machine-done. Or you can redo it better than the original.

I use a kind of knot stitch when I do sail repair and I've never had a repair come loose. They've broken and been cut, but they've never wiggled loose. Push the needle through with the pliers and pull it the rest of the way through with the same pliers (sail material, especially on a thick seam, is hard to get a needle through). Pull the thread through all the way the full length you'll need for the repair and leave a tail on the other side at least as long.

Now go ⅛ inch and push the needle through again, pulling it all the way through and making a tight stitch. Next tie the tail you left the first time with the thread you pulled through on the stitch—just a simple one-loop knot—and then repeat the procedure, tying the tail and bringing it along the stitched seam as you go.

It's not too pretty when you're finished, a little row of knots on the sail, but it's "purely stout and fine," as they used to say, and the seam won't come loose again.

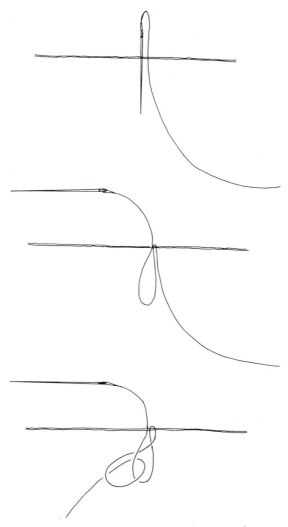

Detail of knot-stitch for sail repair.

SAILING: *From Jibs to Jibing*

Next to a loosened seam in frequency of needing repair is the loosened thread holding other gear on the sail, like a grommet or a slider-holder that goes up the mast. Here, the procedure is easier than sewing the seam. Just redo the sewing as it was done, using the same heavy waxed thread and the pliers to pull the thread through. Leave a long tail and tie a double-knot the first time you loop through, then tie a single knot with each progressive loop. That way it simply can't come loose; each loop has its own independent strength.

Torn sail

With the newer fabrics—especially when they are of the no-tear kind of weave—the torn sail is not as common as it once was. Still, if a sharp object meets a pulled sail, something has to give and it's usually the cloth in the sail.

No matter what the size of the tear the procedure is the same. First, don't just overlap the two edges of the tear and sew them up. This will cause the sail to "pucker" at that point, which in turn will make ripples of cloth go out from the tear. These ripples will harm the smooth curve of the sail, change the movement of air across the sail, and can greatly reduce the efficiency of the sail.

Go to a fabric supply house and get a 2- or 3-square-foot piece of sail-repair material, cloth of the same make and color as your sail. It's good to keep it around, especially if you're doing a lot of hard work with your boat, sailing-camping, etc.

Cut a piece of repair cloth half an inch bigger than the tear all around. Some people cut rectangles or squares, but I always used an oval shape to eliminate messing with corners when I sew.

Lay the patch over the tear and sew all around the outside edge of the patch cloth, using the knot stitch and tying it off when you've gone around. Then refill on thread and sew the two edges of the tear to the patch cloth.

Rubbed sail

Less common on small boats is a hole through the sail caused by constant rubbing. This happens on larger boats, when the sails might work against the rigging, but small boats don't usually have rigging in such a way as to cause problems.

In any case, the repair is much the same as with the torn sail. Cut a piece of repair cloth half an inch bigger than the rubbed-through area all around. Lay this over the worn-through area and sew around the entire patch, using the knot stitch. Then sew back and forth across the worn-out area in an X, using the same knot stitch as you go. If there is a special area that is really bad, you might stitch through that as well. When you're done, take a match (some keep a small candle for this purpose) and melt the ends of the thread in little lumps so they won't unravel.

Burned sails

People will continue to smoke. And there always seems to be some person who comes along and flips an ash on your sail when it's wrapped on the boom. Sails are almost all made of synthetic—plastic-base—material, and when a cigarette ash hits it it melts an instant hole. If it's a large piece of red-hot coal from the end or a flipped cigarette (which happened to me once), it can melt a hole through several layers of sail cloth; my sail had four holes from one cigarette. The sail can also catch on fire, which is why most sailors don't want you smoking around their boat.

The repair is the same as for a tear or a rub. Cut a patch half-inch bigger all around than the burn and sew around it with the knot stitch.

A cautionary note about overall sail repair: don't try shortcuts. Iron-on patches won't hack it. I tried it once.

The same goes for the fabric glues, although they come closer to working than iron-on's. Some people both glue and sew, which is a good policy, but not necessary. If you're going to do it, glue the patch in place with the fabric glue, let it set and dry, then sew, using the knot stitch. *Be absolutely certain you have the right glue.* If you use the wrong glue there is a fair chance you'll melt a big chunk out of your sail; some of the acetone-base glues will just gobble up synthetic fabrics like food. Double-check the glue and make certain it's the right kind for the fabric your sail is made of; if there's any doubt at all, don't use it.

Glue can be a convenient way to position a patch for sewing, but glue is not necessary for repairing sails. It is better to avoid all glue than to use the wrong one.

ROPE REPAIR

It's enough to make old sailors shudder and wince, but the truth of the matter is that with modern ropes, materials, and tight cross-hatch weaving, any old-fashioned concept of rope repair is practically irrelevant.

What makes this doubly sad is that splicing rope was for so many hundreds of years the one thing that all sailors had to know. You will probably never break a modern rope, but if you do or, as is more likely, it wears out from constant use, replace it.

Any attempt at repairing or splicing modern rope almost always meets with failure, and it isn't worth the risk. There may come a moment when you need that rope, and to find out then that the modern weaves and materials won't lend themselves to proper splicing can be worse than disappointing, it can be dangerous.

There is, however, one handy hint to keep in mind. All the modern weaves and fabrics have a disadvantage over the old ropes. They unravel if you even look at them. The cure for this unraveling is to use a match to melt and form the loose ends into clean and tidy lumps. Do this when the rope is new and it will never unravel.

BOAT REPAIR

There are so many different kinds of boats, made of so many different kinds of materials and with so many different parts, that a whole book could be written on boat repair alone. There are many such books in libraries. If you don't find the repair method for your boat in the following section, don't hesitate to use the other sources.

There are many common repair problems caused by hard use and age and they are listed below in their most common order.

Loosened screws

It might seem silly even to discuss something as obvious as a loose screw, but there is more to it than meets the eye.

The repair for loosened screws is to retighten them. (Add a flat-blade and Phillip's screwdriver set to your repair kit.) After you've retightened them about forty times, you begin to look for a way to keep them from coming loose.

There isn't a way to stop the problem entirely. There

are too many stresses and vibrations going on. But there is a way greatly to reduce the frequency of the occurrence.

When a screw starts to loosen up, take it all the way out. Put a sliver of wood down in the hole the screw came out of, cut to fit all the way down inside the hole. (Wooden matches cut off work well for this.) Next, put a dab of glue on the threads of the screw and then put it back in the same hole. The wood sliver will jam it in tighter and the glue will hold it in place. It will still vibrate out, given time, but it will last a lot longer than it would have lasted with no help at all.

You can still take the screw out and put it back in if you have to in the future. The glue won't jam it in so that it won't move, it just holds the wood in place. Avoid using epoxy glues for this as they might glue the screw in place forever.

Worn, damaged (abraded), or rotten wood

Basically the repair is the same for the above listed problems. Sand the wood down very smooth by hand, let it dry *completely*, for days, if possible, to get all possible dampness out of the wood. Then sand once more with very fine paper, then rub with very fine steel wool, and, finally, coat with varnish until it's well filled and sealed, tight, and dry.

It takes a lot of work, but when you're done, there's a good chance that it will never go bad at that place again, unless you hit something or otherwise cause damage.

As with sail repair, don't use shortcuts and don't work to speed up the process. In the long run it will make for more work for you to try and do it fast. Let the wood dry well between coats of varnish, take your time, and you'll only have to do it once.

Broken or shattered wood

There are several approaches to fixing a truly broken piece of wood. Probably the most common method is to get some C-clamps and good waterproof glue. (Buy the glue at a regular hardware store because it will be much cheaper, but make certain that it's a waterproof kind of glue made specifically for wood; the best kind is the one that comes as a powder that you mix up.)

Let the wood dry thoroughly and naturally in the sun or in a warm room until there is absolutely no moisture in it. Then mix the glue as per instructions on the container and glue the pieces together, using the clamps to keep it tight until dry and properly set. No matter how the glue works or what the instructions say, always let the glue dry overnight—or longer, if possible.

When the wood is dry, take the clamps off, sand it with fine paper and steel wool, and varnish or paint the repair to match the rest.

There is a saying about a glued joint that if you did it right, the repair will be stronger than the original

138

wood, and it's true. Now and then though you will come across a break that doesn't lend itself to being glued. Perhaps a seat board breaks straight across the middle, or the tiller handle breaks across the middle. In these two cases glue won't work, because it hasn't the strength to hold on a short joint where there is great stress.

In a case where glue can't be used, it is necessary to make a new piece to replace the old.

Regardless of the piece of wood, or the type, the procedure is the same. Completely remove the broken piece and take it down to the lumber yard and get the same kind of wood to replace the old. If the wood you took out was plywood, get new plywood—made with exterior or waterproof glue—in the same thickness. Don't try to save money and buy thinner wood, because it will just let you down when you least expect it.

When the new piece is cut to fit—you'll find a saber-saw to be perfect for this sort of work—don't put it in yet. Part of what causes rot in wooden boats is making them too fast and not putting a good finish on each board as it's built. Take your time and do it right.

Sand the piece of wood smooth, so smooth that it feels like a piece of glass when rubbed across your cheek.

Then rub it with fine steel wool, and finally, varnish it until it is well filled and sealed on all sides. Do this no matter what the piece of wood is, or how it's to be used on the boat.

Duplicate the broken piece exactly, including any and all holes that must be drilled for screws, then finish the board out with sanding, steel-wooling, and varnishing with varnish or clear plastic finish.

In this way rot won't get a chance to start on it.

Before starting work on a piece of wood, here's a bit of advice. Woodworking is easy and fun, if you have patience and a little knowledge. Pick up a how-to book on woodworking at the library. It doesn't hurt to brush up a bit on your techniques, and thirty minutes of reading might save two hours of frustration later.

Major damage, hull damage, broken mast

There is a feeling in America that if something is really broken, it isn't worth fixing, that it's easier and better to get a new one.

This does *not* hold true with boats. They are always worth fixing, even if they've been run over by a truck.

No matter what the damage, whether slightly serious or catastrophic, the repair is always the same. Take each broken piece out, make a new piece out of exactly the same type of wood purchased from the lumber yard, and put the new one back after finishing properly. If you have any doubt as to what kind of wood it is, take the broken piece with you to the lumber supplier and ask him what it is, then order a new piece. If you can't get a piece—say it's polished teak or something exotic like that—ask the man at the lumber yard what other substitute wood he has that would work. But try for the original kind first.

It is possible to rebuild an entire boat that has been

totally ruined by following the above procedure. In fact, one of the best ways to procure a cheap boat is to call the yacht and boat insurance people in your area and tell them you want a totaled small sailboat. Sooner or later you'll get one. They often fall off cars at high speed, or people back over them. Then take a winter when you can't sail anyway and rebuild the boat piece by piece. (We'll talk about methods for repairing a fiberglass boat in a later section.)

The thing to remember with wood is that the people who made the boat in the first place had to get the wood somewhere and start from scratch. You can do the same.

This procedure includes the hull. If there is a major hole in the hull, don't try to patch it (as you can with glass). Take out the whole piece that is broken and replace it with a new piece that has been properly finished.

If the mast is broken, it can also be replaced. If it's wood take a piece of the broken mast to the lumber yard and order a new mast. It might cost a bit, but it will be far, far cheaper than buying a prefinished new mast.

Remember, duplicate the wood exactly. If it's a wooden mast there will be no knots in it. Be sure the new mast doesn't have any knots to weaken it.

If the mast was aluminum, check with the local aluminum supplier (look in the *Yellow Pages*). Chances are your mast is a straight piece of extruded aluminum from stock. Take the broken one down and order a new one the right length. (It will cost about one tenth as much as ordering one through a regular marine supplier.)

Fiberglass repair

Almost no newer boats are made of wood. While elegant and beautiful, wood is hard to keep up. It takes a lot of maintenance work, and, as they say, all that time varnishing could be spent sailing. One of the advantages of fiberglass, while it's expensive, is its low maintenance.

The other primary advantage—other than the fact that it can't rot—is that it can easily be repaired.

If you have a glass boat, pick up one of those 1-quart cans of fiberglass putty and a square yard of fiberglass cloth and keep them around. Also, get a pair of safety goggles and a respirator-protector mask (the cheap kind made of paper will work). That's all you need to fix almost anything that can go wrong with a fiberglass boat. To make the repair look nice, get a pint of liquid resin with catalyst and keep it on hand with the rest of your material.

When you get a ding or a break or a hole in a glass boat the procedure starts the same as with wood.

Let it dry *thoroughly.* Any moisture content in the broken area will ruin the repair. If at all possible get the boat inside a garage and let it stay there for days to make certain it's completely dried out.

Next, wearing eye and breath protectors and light cloth gloves, clean and sand the broken area. Cut away any shredded or broken glass fibers and get down to solid, cleaned, and sanded material. A little fraying is acceptable, but don't have any long fibers sticking out.

142

The next step depends on the kind of damage that was done. If it's just a crack or bad gouge, fill it with putty, lay a piece of glass cut ¼ inch larger than the damaged area all around on the break, and "paint" over it with one layer of liquid resin when the putty has set up. Let it dry overnight, then use fine sandpaper to sand it down. Repaint it with resin, and repeat resin application and sanding until the surface is as smooth as the original. It will, of course, be clear and you'll be able to see the glass cloth through the resin. If that bothers you, they make a pigment you can buy for the resin, and you can try to match the original color.

If the damage is severe—a hole through the hull—the procedure is changed a bit. You must fix both sides of the break and sandwich the damaged area in new cloth.

You start the same way. Sand, clean, and fill with putty, sanding the surface smooth when it hardens. Then "paint" a layer of cloth cut big enough to cover the hole plus ¼ inch on the inside of the break. Sand and repaint until it is smooth and clean.

Now, on the outside of the break—opposite from where you've finished—do the same thing. Lay a layer of cloth in, paint and repaint with resin until it's smooth, sanding between applications to resmooth it, and when it's completely smooth—so that all the little pockets in the glass are filled and level—you're done. The patch will be stronger than the original hull. While there will be a slightly thickened place in the hull where you did the repair work, the boat will sail as well as before.

SAILING: *From Jibs to Jibing*

This same method can be used to fix a truly horrendous hole, using larger pieces of glass cloth.

No matter what kind of boat you have, the best repair you can do is to prevent the problem in the first place. Sometimes damage is unavoidable, but a good maintenance program will go a long way towards alleviating the repair problems. If you practice good sailing techniques, there is a good chance you'll avoid serious repairs.

Stop problems before they start. Sew up things when they start to go bad, or if you *think* they're going to go bad. If you see a touch of dark spot in wood, sand and refinish it before it can turn to rot. If a seam comes loose, if there's a scratch in the glass, take care of it when you notice it, before it gets out of hand and turns into a full-blown problem.

The old axiom "a stitch in time saves nine" *must* have been about sailing. Except that it should be a stitch in time saves forty-seven, not just nine.

Chapter Fifteen

Using Sailing;
Fine-tuning Your Ability

In modern times sailing has become a sport. Whether people are sailing a small dinghy or going for the America's Cup in a million-dollar boat, it's all a sport. Aside from some special uses (clamming and oystering in the East), the idea of using a sailboat for something other than fun seems pretty much to have gone the way of the clipper ships. When people want to fish they take the outboard, when they want to camp they take the canoe, when they just want to have fun they sail.

Yet one of the true joys of sailing is the flexibility of the boat. Sailing is probably one of the most versatile methods of water travel available—certainly one of the cleanest and cheapest—and yet many people fail to use it. In an age when nonrenewable energy is at a premium, there still seems to be a failure to recognize sailing for what it can be: "free" energy.

As an illustration, the following are two methods of using sailing as something other than just a sport.

SAILING-HIKING-CAMPING

A very simple thought—take your boat and go with the wind. With the exception of parts of the deserts of the Southwest, you can go almost anywhere in North America by water. Indeed, most of the towns and cities in the world are located near some form of waterway, and all you have to do is take advantage of already existing "wet roads."

Take a backpack, and a sleeping bag and lash them in tightly. If you put everything in double-tied plastic garbage sacks it won't get wet even if you capsize. Add some food—as if you were going camping without the boat—and perhaps some fishing gear.

Make sure the weight is in the center of the boat and be sure to file a "flight plan" with somebody before you go, so they'll know where you are. Pay special attention to all safety considerations—remember the life jacket—and off you go.

Here are some tips to make sailing-camping a bit easier.

Try to camp so that when you leave in the morning the wind will be working off shore and carry you out and away easily.

Don't take any chances when you tie up for the night. Tie the boat securely to shore and make certain the sails are down and lashed tightly to the boom so that a sudden

146

night gust won't fill them and take the boat out without you.

If you pull your boat up on shore, be sure to take off the rudder and pull up the centerboard, but also be sure to have them at hand if you need to get under way in a hurry. This is especially true on rivers—any river with a dam—where the water table can rise in a hurry during the night.

If you pull your boat up on shore, it can make a rather nice windbreak for sleeping. But be very careful if you have a fire. Everything on a sailboat is flammable, and it's a long walk home if you burn the boat.

SAILING-FISHING

For thousands of years almost all fishing—personal and commercial—was done from sailing craft. With the advent of engines much of that has died. Yet nothing has really changed.

The wind is still there.

And there are still boats that can sail that wind.

So take your fishing gear sailing with you and give it a try. If you're like me you'll be amazed at how much nicer it is than stinking along with a smudge-pot engine on the stern.

It's so quiet and peaceful that you don't scare the fish. When it comes down to one particular aspect of fishing, it's so much better than engines that it's amazing they ever started using them. When trolling you can control the speed of the boat by pulling in and letting out the sheet. In fact you can get the speed down to a snail's crawl and troll silently over those beds where the fish are normally spooky.

Sailing is a natural for fishing.

FINE-TUNING YOUR SKILLS

No book on sailing can do more than introduce you to the methods, the boat, the wind, and the water. To really get it, you must get in a boat and start sailing. The more you sail the more you'll learn, the more you'll be able to control the boat and yourself.

It is not the purpose of this book to do more than introduce you to sailing. If you wish to race, if you wish to do any lengthy cruising, you must know more than is written here; you must know more than is written in *any* book on sailing.

But there is a general feeling that might help you peak yourself on sailing—fine-tune your abilities.

As you sail, as you practice, remember that the wind, the boat, the water, and you are one entity. You can't separate any of the elements and sail well.

When you turn a sailboat the rudder doesn't merely act on the water to wheel the boat around, the way it does under power. Instead, it is a function of the wind on the sail, the keel, the water density, your hand on the keel, your weight in the boat—all of that must be right for a sailboat to turn correctly.

You can jack it around the corner, as they say, and come out the other side like a sailing brick, or you can feel the wind and water and yourself as part of them and swoop around like a gull wheeling in the air.

If you want to learn how to sail, sail as much as you can and work to become part of it. Learn to dance with the wind and the water.

Bibliography

Colgate, Stephen. *Colgate's Basic Sailing Theory*. New York: Van Nostrand Reinhold Co., 1973.

George, M. B. *Basic Sailing*. New York: Motor Boating.

Gibbs, Tony. *Practical Sailing*. New York: Motor Boating.

Farnham, Moulton H. *Sailing for Beginners*. New York: Macmillan, 1967.

Glossary

Abeam. Straight off to the side of the middle of the boat

Aboard. On the boat

Aft. The rear of the boat

Aground. To run up on shallow bottom; to get stuck

Anchor. Hook for fastening the boat to the bottom

Batten. Stick for stiffening the edge of the sail

Beam. Fattest part of the boat; widest part at the middle

Beam Reach. Sailing direcly across the wind

Bearing. Direction to go: i.e., bearing to the east, bearing to the west

Beat. To tack against the wind; beat to windward

Block. Pulley

Boom. Long stick to the side of the mast, spar, for attaching the bottom of the sail

Bow. Front of the boat

Capsize. Flip over

Cast off. To untie from the dock

Centerboard. Blade that sticks down through the center of the boat and acts to keep it on course

Cleat. Horned device for attaching rope; i.e., for tying off boat or sail

153

Glossary

Current. Movement of water

Daggerboard. Type of centerboard

Dinghy. Small sailing boat

Downhaul. Small rope for tightening or pulling down on the sail

Downwind. Moving with the wind

Fall off. To let the nose of the boat fall off with the movement of wind

Foresail. Forward sail on a two-sail boat; i.e., the jib

Gunwale. Edge of the boat

Halyard. Rope for hoisting sail

Head up. To head up into the wind

Heel. To tip with the movement of the wind

Helm. Steering handle

Hike. To get up on the edge of the boat to counteract the heeling motion.

In irons. Caught with your nose in the wind and not moving

Jib. Front sail. See *foresail*

Jibe. To turn the boat when sailing downwind to flop the wind on the opposite side of the sail

Jib sheet. Rope controlling the jib sail

Keel. Center rib of the boat; main backbone

Ketch. Two-masted boat with small mast in the rear

Knot. Unit of speed measurement; a knot is one nautical mile per hours (6080 feet)

Leeway. Move to the downwind side

Luff. Slapping of sail when it's loose in the wind

Mainsail. Main sail on two-sail boat

154

Mizzen. Small rear sail on ketch
Outhaul. Line for pulling sail out along boom
Point. Ability of a boat to move into the wind
Port. Left
Reach. To sail across the wind
Secure. To tie up
Sheet. Rope or line to tie off sail
Sloop. Single mast sailboat with two sails
Starboard. Right
Stern. Rear of boat
Stow. To put things away
Tack. To sail at an angle to the wind
Tiller. Handle for steering. See *helm*
Windward. The direction of the wind

Index

ABOUT THE AUTHOR

Gary Paulsen was raised in Minnesota on a farm adjacent to the immense northern wilderness areas. He has published many articles, T.V. scripts, and dozens of books on a wide variety of subjects, including fiction. One of his favorite subjects is the wilderness and its denizens. Paulsen and his family reside in a home in northern Minnesota that he built from scratch where one can still see herds of deer foraging through the pine thickets.